LINCOLN CHRISTIAN COLLEGE A   P9-BXY-994

Growing
Through an Effective
Church School

D0002758

Growing
Through an Effective Church School

Frank Proctor

CBP Press
St. Louis, Missouri

© 1990 CBP Press

All rights reserved. No part of this book may be reproduced without the publisher's written permission. Address: CBP Press, Box 179, St. Louis, MO 63166.

Unless otherwise indicated, all scripture quotations are from the Revised Standard Version of the Bible, copyrighted 1946, 1952, © 1971, 1973 by the Division of Christian Education of the National Council of Churches of Christ in America.

Quotations marked TEV are from the *Good News Bible*. Old Testament: Copyright © American Bible Society 1976. New Testament: Copyright © American Bible Society 1966, 1971, 1976. Used by permission.

Library of Congress Cataloging in Publication Data

Proctor, Frank.
  Growing through an effective church school / /Frank Proctor.
      p. cm
  ISBN: 0-8272-1235-6
  1. Sunday-schools—Growth. 2. Church growth. I. Title.
BV1523.G75P76 1990
268—dc20   89-27522-
                                                         CIP

Printed in the United States of America

Contents

83723

Introduction:
Stepping Stones to a
Growing Church School

The Christian church today faces both a major crisis and a significant opportunity. The crisis is evidenced by the continuing decline of attendance in the Sunday school. The opportunity is for the church school to grow and rebuild itself, as so many indicators now suggest is possible if the church school can truly be prepared.

For such a time as this the church must be better equipped to share its word of truth and hope to a world that is looking for spiritual direction. It is the ministry of Christian education that is best suited to equip the church to fulfill its mission of leading people to understand and adopt the Christian faith.

I have been involved in the ministry of Christian education for over twenty years, having served on the staff of congregations with various church school enrollments. I have spent countless hours preparing and conducting workshops to train church school administrators and staff members in how to do their jobs better. I have advised teachers on how to make their lessons more interesting and more useful to the personal lives of their students. I have written magazine articles about numerous issues in Christian education. Until 1986 I had never attended nor conducted a workshop on *how to increase church school attendance*.

When leading workshops on Christian education, I was often asked, "How can we get more children and youth to attend our Sunday school?" and, "What can we do to get more people involved?" I had no good answers. So my usual advice was to suggest that a well-planned lesson by an effective teacher and a full program of educational activities in the church may help attendance to grow.

Without knowing for sure, I had to admit that such work just may not help increase attendance. I assumed that if a lesson were exciting enough, students would naturally invite their friends; if our programs were well suited to meet people's needs, the world would automatically discover the fact and start attending our church school. Now we know that someone has to make more intentional efforts if there is to be any growth in the church school.

As a consultant, I was only prepared to train teachers to develop leaders for the church school and to plan effective programs but not to build up the church school attendance. When challenged by the growth of the Sunday school in other denominations, I could only suggest that "quality is more important than quantity." As a matter of fact, I have now come to realize that such either/or thinking (quality vs. quantity), and having to choose one or the other, can actually be a barrier to growth.

Like most mainline Protestant Christian education professionals, I was concentrating on following Christ's command to "Go and teach" while ignoring the importance of that same command to "Make disciples." Lacking further insight, I would usually try to avoid the issue entirely. After so many years of hearing the same request for help, I finally began to realize that, indeed, the questions I sought to avoid were the *most* important ones for the church to be asking today. Christian educators should have been seeking the answers to such questions:

"How do we get more people to join our church school?"

"How can we do that in a way that is consistent with the best educational theory and our understanding of the claims of the gospel?"

These are important questions!

I began to explore this concern with my colleagues. Together we discovered that there are very few resources available in current Christian education materials that provide guidance or suggestions for increasing church school attendance.

After having done some research in the church growth literature and asking teachers and administrators a lot of questions, I am convinced that there are some useful insights now available for our use. This book is an effort to share some of those new insights with you.

"How do we increase church school attendance?" is one of the most important questions for Christian education today. When we ask this we are assuming that *the primary task of Christian education* is:

(1) to lead (educate) people to acknowledge and understand their faith,
(2) to bring people into the community of the faith—the church,
(3) to encourage them to adopt the lifestyle of committed disciples,
(4) to enable them to accept full responsibility as leaders in the church.

Christian education is not a self-sufficient ministry in the church, independent of or indifferent to all other ministries. Its historic partnership with evangelism has broken down in the modern age of the church. The issue is further confused when the task of evangelism is defined too narrowly. It is too limited when evangelism is seen only as recruiting new members into the church or church school and/or simply as "bringing persons to a saving knowledge of Jesus Christ," as is so often stated. The task of Christian education is also too limited when it is defined in narrow terms. The purposes and tasks of Christian education and evangelism are overlapping and in many ways even identical. It is time to renew that partnership for the sake of the church.

The *principles of church growth*, as suggested by many current authors, provide us some very effective tools for accomplishing the educational and evangelical mission of the church and the church school. Yet, *the way we do mission and education says who we are as a church.* Some may be inclined to apply church growth principles in a manner that betrays what the church is truly called to be and to do. When a congregation tries to recruit newcomers by awarding bicycles, or television sets, or candy bars, it models the wrong vision of what the church is. The church is a servant, and those who join its community accept their own servanthood. Church growth principles must be faithful to that servanthood, just as the educational standards must be faithful.

Behind the question, "*How* are we to increase the attendance in our church school?" lies the more important and comprehensive question, "*Why* do we seek to increase that attendance?" It is not for "success," nor for "survival," not to have a more exciting program than our competitor churches, not to be more educationally effective. We must *make disciples.* That is why Christian education must work to increase the number of church school attenders by inviting the unchurched. It is essential to being faithful to our vocation. Let us be *responsible evangelists* as well as responsible educators.

This book is designed to address the major issues that effect the growth of the church through its church school. It is unlike most other books on this subject as it discusses growth principles for each age level.

The first portion of the book seeks to set a framework and philosophy of the ministry of Christian education.

The second part of the book provides the practical applications of church growth principles for each age level served by the ministry of education.

The author is deeply indebted to a great many people for the inspiration to pursue the writing of this book. There has been a "great crowd of witnesses" who have been my mentors in this vocation of religious education. I especially acknowledge my colleague, Linda Chenoweth, who did so much to help me research the background for this book.

I want to thank my supportive family, particularly my loving wife, Nola, for their patience and encouragement throughout the years of the production of this manuscript.

The real test for Christian education in the mainline churches over the next few years will be whether or not they can energetically build on the foundation of a heritage of two hundred years and whether or not they can find effective ways to bring new disciples into the faith.

This book is written on the assumption that an effective Christian education program will by definition also be a growing one and that a declining church school is probably not fully faithful to its true educational vocation. It is written to provide some real *stepping stones to church school growth.*

1

A New Day Is Dawning
for the Church School

Said Alice to the Cheshire Cat, "Please tell me which path to choose."
"Where are you going?" asked the Cat.
"I don't know. Can't you tell I am lost?" replied Alice.
"Then it really doesn't matter which way you go, does it?"
—Alice in Wonderland

"Go therefore and make disciples of all nations . . . teaching them to observe all that I have commanded you. . . ."
—Matthew 28:19, 20

The church school has enjoyed a long and cherished history, with many proud moments. Even though the past few years have seen a drop in enrollment and attendance, the church school remains the largest single educational enterprise in this country. More adults are enrolled in the church's school than in all other educational programs and institutions. A new decade is dawning that promises another proud chapter for the church school if we meet the challenge of this great moment of opportunity.

The Sunday school has been very important to those who have shared its history. Those adults who at some time in their lives have attended Sunday school have very fond memories of loving, caring

11

teachers. Every church school teacher wishes that the pupils placed in his or her charge could be challenged by the teaching to live their lives more like God would have them live. All leaders in the Christian education movement hope that pupils will learn more about their faith and will make moral decisions that are fully attuned to the Spirit of God and the teachings of the Bible.

The modern Sunday school movement began over two hundred years ago with rather humble beginnings. It emphasized basic reading, writing, and character development. In the late nineteenth and early twentieth centuries it had phenomenal growth in America, and its primary emphasis was on evangelism and basic lay studies of the Bible. In the 1930s and, culminating in the 1950s, the Sunday school experienced a virtual explosion of growth, featuring a well-rounded, age-level developed, Bible-based curriculum that utilized the finest educational methods available.

Then in the 1960s and 1970s there began a significant decline in enrollment and attendance, while the Sunday school changed its emphasis to the nurture of Christian families and to teaching ways to live a Christian life in a contemporary world. Throughout its glorious history and its recent discouraging decline, the Sunday school planted the seeds for what can be a hopeful future. The evidence suggests that this future will bring another era of growth if it is ready to respond to this present challenge.

The urgent mission that now confronts the Sunday school is for it to be able to glean the greatest resources from its heritage and at the same time to adopt the newest insights from theology and the social sciences. This will enable it to respond to the opportunities presented by this decade—indeed, the emerging new century.

"What Has Happened to the Church School? Nobody Attends Anymore."

Many people are asking this perplexing question. When they look at the attendance today, comparing it with their memories of the 1950s or even earlier years, they wonder why things have changed so much. When they walk down the halls of all but the newest congregations and glance into the classrooms that were once filled with children, they find many of the rooms standing vacant. Few rooms are being used and even in those used, the number of pupils seems to be small. Where have the pupils gone?

Many church school leaders complain that they cannot get people to volunteer to be teachers anymore. Those who do agree to serve are sometimes apathetic or discouraged. The commitment and inspiration that characterized our church school and its teachers so many years ago no longer seem to exist. Where have all the good teachers gone?

Critics assert that the Sunday school has been sorely neglected. Some blame the volunteer teachers. Others accuse the clergy or church staffs. Others blame the national leadership of the denominations for such neglect. Some complain that the curriculum is no longer helpful or effective in teaching the Bible. Why is the Sunday school is such disarray? Why have church leaders given up on the Sunday school?

Other people hear about the lively church schools in new suburban parishes or some of the congregations of the evangelical wing of the church. They wonder why their own mainline congregation has suffered such losses when others seem to flourish. They may be tempted to conclude that they are the only church to have a declining Sunday school.

Some people complain that children are different today: Some are so ill-behaved that many adults refuse to teach in the Sunday school. Still others blame lazy parents for not insisting that their children attend Sunday school. Divorce and broken homes make it difficult for single parents to keep up regular attendance. Children are often visiting their other parents on weekends and are not taken to church by those parents. Why does it seem that parents no longer feel that they need to take their children to Sunday school?

It is true that most denominations and many congregations in this country have experienced substantial decline in church membership and in Sunday school attendance. In fact, for most, the decline in Sunday school attendance has progressed at a rate two times as fast as the drop in church membership or worship attendance.

But the times are changing. We are at the threshold of the turnaround, a new beginning. The rate of decline is being reduced, and in many areas growth is beginning to show. Most denominations are beginning to see the bottom of the pendulum swing of church school attendance. An upswing is in the making. The annual yearbook of the churches published by the National Council of Churches in America confirms this trend. In 1982 the Missouri Synod Lutheran Church saw its first year of growth in the attendance in church school after fifteen years of decline. The 1983 church membership figures showed an increase in the Presbyterian Church in America (4.31 percent) and in the Episcopal church (.02 percent). Other denominations who reported increases include The Southern Baptists, the Assembly of God, The Roman Catholic Church, The Church of God, and the Mennonites. The United Methodist Church reported in 1986 that the drop in attendance figures slowed and that even a slight increase was experienced. The Disciples of Christ and the United Church of Christ discovered that the rate of their church membership decline was reduced to less than 1 percent in 1985 (the best news in twenty years).[1] In 1986 The Christian Church (Disciples of Christ) reported increased total church school enrollments over 1985 in twenty-one of its thirty-six regions in the U.S. and Canada.[2]

Some Popular Reasons Given for the Recent Decline

The rise of television and the increased mobility in the family that began in the 1950s made a significant change in people's lifestyles. For some families it meant that the church school was no longer needed as the primary social center in their lives. They began to substitute other social settings for church attendance.

The social unrest of the sixties and the seventies is blamed for causing people to lose faith in the church. Even church leaders were taking radical political positions. It appeared to some that they were abandoning the church's main purpose, which they saw as the spiritual development of Christians. Some felt that the Sunday school materials spent too much time dealing with social justice, wars, drugs, and conflict over civil rights and too little time talking about biblical faith. This caused some people to reject the church and its message.

Some people have blamed the drop in church school attendance on the many changes in curriculum. Over and over the denominational publishing companies have revised their materials, using the newest educational methodologies, and yet many church school teachers feel the resources are still unusable in their congregations.

The sexual revolution, with its impact on traditional family life, was an enormous detriment to the Sunday school. Some people think this led parents to cease caring about the church or about religious training for their children. Other parents are so permissive that they fail to teach discipline to their children. Some parents reject the church's teaching about personal morals, feeling it is too restrictive or Victorian.

There Is a Better Explanation

People commonly believe that the changes listed above are the major reasons for the Sunday school decline. But no one has really been able to measure the power of their impact. On the other hand, there are some other forces at work that do explain some of the decline.

The busy schedules of families in which both parents work puts a strain on its members. Many mothers employed outside the home are no longer willing to give the effort to volunteer to be Sunday school teachers. Many parents, tired after working a forty-hour job (career professionals work even more hours), want to use Sundays as a day to sleep in or to spend needed time with family.

Another result of the social revolution in family life and changing sex roles was a much lowered birthrate between 1965 and 1978. Because many young women delayed their time of childbearing until after they received college degrees and had established their own personal careers, significantly fewer babies were born in those years. Elementary schools, high schools, and colleges felt the enormous impact of such a decline in the total number of children born in those years.

The list of reasons given for the decline also includes:

(a) many clergy felt that Christian education was a "childish" activity; (b) many lost faith in the ability of the church school to teach Christian behavior and were convinced it had only become a comfortable social club; (c) most of the women who had been a major source for professional leadership in the Sunday school as directors of Christian education chose to avoid the professional ministry of education and pursued preaching as their career goal as clergy.

Most of these forces were so powerful that no amount of commitment or energetic efforts by even the best churches were able to reverse the trends. Still, the Sunday school and its corps of dedicated workers kept hard at their task with committed service. They made every effort to apply creative responses to such rapid social changes.

It is important to realize that these trends—these forces for decline—have had only a short life when compared to the entire history of the Sunday school. Even today, there are many signs that lead us to believe we are ready for a period of new growth in the church.

Hope for the Church School—A Look at Our Heritage

Let us look beyond the changes of the most recent decades, with their conditions over which we had little or no control. Let us review the whole history of the Sunday school to gain a broader perspective. By doing so we may discover some insights that can help us improve the Sunday school today.

The first Sunday school was founded over two hundred years ago in England by Robert Raikes. Every weekend he saw many young children roaming the streets and alleys of London. They were forced to work long hours in the factories; but on the weekends they ran wild with little supervision. Parents were often victims of alcoholism and gave little attention to training or discipline for their children.

Seeking to improve the lot of those children, Raikes brought them each Sunday into a healthy environment and then gave them some moral and religious training. The Bible was used as a simple textbook to teach reading and to train the children about morals and character. The first Sunday schools were started not so much for education, or even for evangelism, but as a social service to the poor.

The whole idea of Sunday school was quickly adopted by other industrialists and many new schools were started. Teachers were hired. Churches were first approached with requests to use their facilities to house the Sunday schools. Some responded; others refused. At first there was little clergy involvement. In fact, some even vigorously opposed the spread of the Sunday school, fearing the growing power of its lay leaders and assuming the laity could not properly teach the Bible.

The Sunday school found a natural home in America. Charles Wesley was a prime mover in its introduction. It was imported to America primarily as an educational venture. The church has always valued education, especially in the New World. In fact, the first reader to gain much popularity was the *New England Primer,* which even taught the alphabet (and reading) with "A—in Adam all Die . . ." to "Z—Zachariah he did . . . ." Churches established schools to teach their own children basic reading, writing, and arithmetic, as well as the central religious doctrines of each community.

In the late 1800s the Sunday school easily attached itself to the Great Awakening, the revivalism movement, and thus identified itself more closely with an evangelistic purpose. As the population centers of this country moved west, Sunday schools were often started in new communities even before congregations or churches were organized.

As early as 1846, Horace Bushnell identified the controversy over the objective of the Sunday school—whether it should be for conversion or for nurture. There were statewide and national conventions to which Sunday school teachers from all denominations traveled many miles in order to be trained how to teach the Bible and how to bring nonbelievers into the church.

The Uniform Lesson Series was developed by an interdenominational organization, the Sunday School Union, a forerunner of the educational departments of the National Council of Churches. Every class studied the same biblical text on any given Sunday, and within a six-year cycle all had studied the teachable scriptures in the entire Bible. The rapid growth of inexpensive publishing allowed curriculum, study guides, and weekly magazines or take home papers to be rapidly produced and easily circulated.

In the 1900s even church architecture was significantly influenced by the Sunday school movement. Many church buildings were designed in that era on "the Akron Plan." When the family arrived at the church for Sunday school parents would take their preschooler to the cradle roll room or kindergarten room in the basement, then climb the stairs to the church's sanctuary, where all the pews were fashioned in semicircles. There all ages met together for the "Opening Exercises." An entirely new hymnody developed for use in the Sunday school. Several rituals appeared for celebrating people's birthdays and for taking up an offering that belonged entirely to the Sunday school or for world missions.

After a kind of keynote presentation by the Sunday school superintendent, the classes all moved to their own assigned areas around the outside of the sanctuary. Rolling partitions were moved into place, and the class lessons begun. Usually all adults, regardless of age, were separated into two classes: The Men's Bible Class and The Women's Bible Class.

It was quite common for the teachers of the large adult groups to be well-known community leaders. Great names such as John Wanamaker, H.J. Heinz, the Colgates, and many others became well known across the country for their leadership in the Sunday school. This was primarily a lay-led organization, and the clergy were often jealous of its activity. Denominational publishing houses were founded about this time.

In the 1910s and 1920s there was a tendency for each Sunday school leader to train his or her own successor. National Sunday school conventions became more related to specific denominations.

The national offices of those denominations began to recruit and hire professional educators to help the Sunday school. Age level distinctions were instituted in the curriculum by these professionals, and the Sunday school grew.

In the 1940s greater attention was given to the educational methods gleaned from the expertise of the public school system. These were employed in the designing and writing of curriculum. Many congregations began to employ second staff persons—often as directors of religious education.

At the same time, there had already begun a minor revolution in public education after the Great Depression. For the first time junior high and even high school diplomas were a desired achievement for all people—not those few who were college bound. Sunday school and church enrollments continued to increase.

The dawning of the 1950s began what might truly be called the "Golden Age of the Sunday School." Just after the conclusion of World War II and the Korean Conflict, before television began to have such a powerful influence over popular culture, there was a great explosion of new families and new houses and new churches in new suburbs. New educational buildings were being built for long established congregations as well as for churches in the new neighborhoods.

As the population began to develop around new growing suburbs, the churches began to reflect that new identity. New public school districts were growing as fast as the suburbs, and even rural districts were consolidated to enhance the educational resources for all children. People felt optimistic about all of life and were joining almost every service organization: Kiwanis, Lions, Rotary, Masons, Boys Scouts, Girl Scouts. People were joining churches in much the same spirit that led them to join the other groups.

More and more churches were remodeling their existing Sunday school classrooms to fit new understandings of age level needs for children and youth, or were building all new units. Each church developed a thriving youth program plus several children's choirs, and probably sponsored a Scout troop.

More and more adults were added to the Sunday school and were influenced by their generation's appetite for learning. Colleges were bursting at the seams with returning servicemen who were attending on the benefits of the G.I. Bill. In those churches that previously had a weekly midweek Bible study led by the pastor, new classes and courses were added to the Sunday morning menu for adults. Some congregations began to have two worship services with concurrent Sunday schools. For some families this meant children were in Sunday school while adults attended the worship service. A new attitude began to emerge unnoticed by most church leaders: Adults were beginning to think the Sunday school was primarily for children while adults went to the worship services. This concept was reinforced in those denominations that also had a strong tradition of confirmation for adolescents. Their children no longer were encouraged to attend Sunday school after they were confirmed.

More educational resources were produced by the national offices of the denominations. These often included new curricula that reflected greater denominational loyalty than was the case before.

About this time religious education professionals began to reject the "old fashioned" ideas and methods for the Sunday school and even insisted upon the adoption of a new name: *the church school*. Great debates occurred over the "evils" of the older "Sunday school" with its attendance charts and opening exercises, and the "outmoded" understanding of a daily vacation Bible school. They argued that the summer vacation school need not always meet daily and that it need not necessarily study the Bible but should teach about the church. Despite this new attempt at a greater sophistication in educational method, most lay people could not remember to make the appropriate changes in their language; it did not seem so important to them.

Each church was able to have an active youth program, for the church still served as the cultural and social programming unit for most communities. These youth organizations became more aligned to a particular denomination. Even as people became more mobile in metropolitan areas, young families that had moved into the suburbs were still likely to travel back to the neighborhood church where they had grown up and where their parents were still members.

In the 1960s denominations were coming to understand that the separations between them were unnecessarily artificial. The call to ecumenism encouraged many denominations to enter into the production of a new shared curriculum. For the most part it encouraged more liberal, free thinking in its educational method as well as its content.

This time also brought a new understanding of the role of leaders in the church. Many educational professionals felt that the older style of Sunday school was entirely too concerned with minute details of organizational structure. There were far too many minor offices that had to be filled with inexperienced people who really did not understand sound educational practices. So the Sunday school organization was replaced with one more closely aligned with the congregation's other decision-making structures. In some churches, the Sunday school superintendent, as the primary leader of the educational program, was replaced by the chair of the education department or council. The Sunday school department and the individual classes were encouraged to give up their own bank accounts and merge with a unified budget of the entire congregation.

Most people in the Sunday school movement during the late 1960s may remember it as the time of new curriculum. This curriculum gave more emphasis to understanding the radical social upheaval that was then taking place, forcing people to ask serious questions about their role in society. To many experienced teachers in the Sunday school this seemed to be abandoning Bible teaching for some new form of the "social gospel," against which they had fought so many years before.

The decade of the 1970s saw the harvest of the fruits of the radical changes begun in the 1960s. All fraternal organizations and service groups began to decline in their memberships. The institutions that held American society together were losing their influence—the school, the government, and the church. The mainline churches began their most rapid period of decline.

The decade of the 1970s was also one of self-absorption. Many people were introduced to various psychologies and Eastern religions that practiced new and different religious rituals. Transcendental meditation replaced Bible study and prayer groups for many people.

The prevalent concepts of learning, with their emphasis on small groups, begun in the sixties, utilized the insights of psychology and sociology for understanding group processes. They made their way from the training of professional leaders into the church school of congregations impacting on resources, teaching styles, and class structures. The lecture method of teaching was often replaced by a group discussion format in which all persons were encouraged to share the leadership.

The new curriculum was judged by many to be too difficult for most volunteer teachers to teach well. It required more knowledge-able teachers and more preparation time. So there developed a whole new group of independent consultants and publishing groups that serviced mainline churches. The two best known of these groups were the National Teacher Education Project, headed by Locke Bowman out of Scottsdale, Arizona, and the Griggs Educational Service headed by Donald and Patricia Griggs, later joined to Abingdon Press.

The1970s also held the seeds of a growing desire by many persons to recapture the traditional values in their own lives and for their families. Independent of any congregation, many began to develop their own home Bible study groups. These groups were often in partnership with the newest evangelistic thrust known as the "Lay Witness Mission." Sometimes the Sunday school was the target of the witnessing by many of this movement's followers. Some would tell their story with a testimony like: "I had attended Sunday school and church all my life, but not until this experience did I ever really know Jesus as my Lord." While such testimonies were genuine and helpful to some people, they provoked a strong negative reaction from church educators who saw such comments as a repudiation of their ministry. Such experiences had the result of increasing the antagonism between Christian education and Christian evangelism.

The 1980s were a mixture of several different developments. The rapid inflation of the 1970s was not matched with growth of financial stewardship in the churches. Church schools had fewer needs for curriculum because they had fewer participants. When this decline was paired with the growing frustration about the new curriculums, great financial distress was felt by many denominational headquarters and their publishing institutions. In fact, several mainline denominations sold their presses and got out of the business of printing.

The 1980s also brought the breakup of several ecumenical alliances for Christian education. The growing appetite for more conservative values in the society at large was coupled with a growing volume of materials from independent, conservative publishing groups. In declining Sunday schools, separate age levels were merged. A new need for curriculum that was prepared for smaller classes of adults and children became apparent. This called for materials that were more "broadly graded" or more usable in classes in which a broader age span was included. The image of the Sunday school as a large institution in the metropolitan or suburban setting with many children, many adults, lots of teachers, and many classrooms was replaced with the expectation that most churches would have small classes, inexperienced teachers, and only a few children.

Hope for the Church School—The Present Climate

Now here we are in the last decade of the twentieth century. Several important changes suggest this is a time for new hope for the Sunday school.

The slump in the birthrate that characterized the1970s was replaced with a new baby boom in the 1980s. The women who delayed childbearing in the late sixties and early seventies now began to have children. In the same years a new group of the baby boom generation also began having its children at the customary time—at ages eighteen to twenty-five. As a result we now have a double group of young children (from infants to about age ten) showing up at our schools and Sunday schools. Most school districts in the country are now having difficulties finding enough classrooms for all this influx of younger children because the economics of the earlier decade and the reduction in the number of children had encouraged them to sell their classrooms and the extra school space.

The Gallup Organization now tells us that the parents of these younger children are quite apt to bring their children to our church schools because they have a strong wish to provide religious and moral training for their children. This desire seems stronger than has been the case for over three decades.

Most demographers, those who help us plan for the future based upon population data, are telling us that in the next few years our society will become more and more "family" oriented because many of the couples who were previously childless are now making decisions that include not just personal appetites but family needs. Corporations are learning that they must provide child care and arrange for parent leave at the time of birth as well as leaves provided for parents to stay home from work to nurse a sick child. The entertainment and restaurant industry is planning fewer "yuppy" restaurants and singles resorts. They will be replaced with family entertainment centers and vacation packages that appeal to families.

The other major age group in our population that continues to grow at a rapid rate is composed of people over sixty-five. The popular media, government reports, and our own personal experience in the church tell us that most people are living longer into their mature years with better health. Adults are able to function as effective leaders in our churches at much older ages than was the case even as recently as twenty-five years ago. These people are apt to be good prospects for our evangelistic and educational programs if we are sensitive to their spiritual needs and the kinds of transitions they experience as they mature.

A recent poll conducted by *Better Homes and Gardens* also demonstrated that the people of America have a stronger desire to define their lives in spiritual terms than is often believed to be the case in American culture. Sunday schools in this decade have begun to slow the decline in attendance, and for some churches there has even begun to be an increase.[3]

Conclusion

Many respected thinkers in the church today and those who watch the social, economic, and political trends of our society tell us there is dawning a new day of growth and renewal for the Sunday school. The times are changing (again), and the changes appear to be quite hopeful for the church. Lyle Schaller has called it a "Contemporary Religious Revival."[4]

The ministry of Christian education must be prepared to capitalize on this moment in time. It has the broad experience needed. The church school has the apparatus, the structure, and the tools. What must we do to take advantage of this present opportunity? In this book we will suggest what can be done. We have collected the knowledge from many different sources in order to suggest some stepping stones that should work.

A glorious heritage of the Sunday school movement informs and equips us to work effectively. The present age and its current appetite for spiritual meaning in life empower us to take advantage of the present opportunities. The gospel mandate to "Go therefore and make disciples . . . teaching them to observe all that I have commanded you" (Matthew 28:19, 20) demands that we take our job seriously and fulfill our mission enthusiastically.

Restoring the Partnership of Education and Evangelism

For it is by our faith that we are put right with God; it is by our confession that we are saved.

—Romans 10:10, TEV

Education without evangelism makes Pharisees; evangelism without education makes fanatics.

—George Sweazy[1]

... until we find a place for evangelism and conversion within our educational ministry, the church's educational mission will remain impotent.

—John H. Westerhoff, III[2]

The major reason for the decline of the Sunday school in the mainline denominations is the abandonment of a commitment to evangelism as central to the church school's responsibility and mission.

Unfortunately, many educators and Sunday school leaders tend to dichotomize the "educational ministry" from the "evangelistic ministry." And it is this distinction that is the root of most stagnant/declining Sunday schools. . . . The most important issue in moving a Sunday school forward in growth *is a clear purpose that reflects the mission and priority of Christ.* Without such a purpose, a Sunday school will flounder, turn inward toward "maintenance," become exclusively nurture-oriented, and eventually stagnate and decline.[3]

This kind of turning inward has been present in all the areas of Christian education.

In recent years Christian education scholars and those who design curriculum and resources and plan for leadership training for the Sunday school have neglected to address the role of evangelism and its call for students of the church school for initial conversion and membership in the church. This is no longer included as a central ingredient in either the content or the goals of the church's educational mission. There are very few—in fact almost no—guidelines in the curriculum manuals for making Christian education more evangelistic. The teachers' manuals list no activities designed to help a teacher know how to increase attendance, how to teach the pupils to "proclaim the word of God" to the unchurched, nor how to invite them to join the church and to adopt its faith. This neglect fosters a separation of the ministry of education and of the ministry of evangelism.

There often develops within congregations a kind of controversy between leaders of the church school and the leaders charged with evangelism and outreach. Sometimes there is criticism; at other times there is competition for time and attention of the church for limited financial resources.

The Sunday school must restore the partnership that existed in the early history of the Sunday school movement if it is to remain vital and if it is ever to expect to be able to grow.

A Simple Definition

It is tempting to begin this discussion by raising the argument that has been raging for some time over an accurate definition of evangelism, one that is comprehensive enough for today's church. But for the purposes of this discussion, a simple definition of conversion and evangelism should be adequate. *Evangelism is the*

*work of the church as it proclaims the rule of God and God's
coming kingdom on earth so that individuals will hear and
respond in commitment to a new life of discipleship.* Their
response (conversion) can be shaped by educational processes
(nurture that encourages maturation), or by immediate personal
experiences that produce new convictions, or by the community at
worship. Yet conversion, the individual's response, generally follows
a three-step process: (1) hearing and coming to an initial understanding of the claims the gospel makes upon one's own personal life; (2)
a decision or a growing commitment to adopt that claim for oneself
in such a way that it shapes all one's subsequent decisions and lifestyle;
and (3) a conscious identification with the church as a community of
persons who believe the claims of the gospel.

This definition may not describe the entire arena in which
persons become transformed by the claims of the gospel or in which
persons gradually grow into a conscious awareness that they are
Christian. Still, when we talk about conversion, commitment, or
evangelism in this chapter we basically mean this process that involves
both teacher (or evangelist) and student (or disciple). In this task,
evangelism and Christian education are a true partnership.

How Did the Partnership Begin to Dissolve?

In the ancient church, Christian education and evangelism were
synonymous. The primary education work of the church was preparing the catechumens (the candidates for Christianity) to join the
church. These candidates were trained for a number of years. The
process included listening to many sermons, asking questions, re-
sponding to many questions. It included very rich and dramatic rituals
of induction, culminating with an all-night vigil on Saturday night
before Easter as a reenactment of the resurrection. John Westerhoff
has helped educators by recalling that ancient tradition. He suggests
that we should see the whole faith community as the embodiment of
the content of faith. The rituals we celebrate as well as some we might
re-adopt are the best teachers of the faith.

The recent history of the Sunday school, especially since the
middle 1940s, shows the most apparent separation between education and evangelism. But the modern separation was begun much
earlier. Around the turn of the century when the popular revivalism
movement was sweeping this country, some of the leaders of the

Christian education movement had begun to be influenced by the theology of the liberal "social gospel" school. Scholars such as George Coe and Horace Bushnell began to write that the purpose of Christian education was to prepare people to live in the world and not simply for an emotional response to the revivalists' invitation. They recognized that most persons were coming to a basic commitment to Christ and the church through the normal maturation process of growing up in the family of the church. This commitment to Christ grew out of experience but was controlled by learned information. These thinkers adopted the term *nurture* as a more clear meaning of the purpose of Christian education for the new age.

At this same period John Dewey was having a profound influence on the development of all educational theory by showing that students learn faster and retain more through their experience than they do through mere rote memory. Hence, materials began to show that people learn faster by doing than by hearing or memorizing.

The American Sunday School Union, which had been functioning for many decades, was already having strong reactions to the new theological liberalism evidenced in such actions as the introduction into the curriculum of biblical criticism. They saw this new development as another attack on the traditional message of the Sunday school. From this point the differences became more and more apparent. The Sunday School Union saw evangelism as one of its primary goals, while the followers of Bushnell and Coe advocated "nurture" as a more appropriate style for religious education

Most local congregations were not aware of these differences, and so they kept the traditional rituals and methods of the old Sunday school movement. Yet, most of the curriculum materials they had to use were being developed from the new educational philosophy adopted by the more liberal Religious Education Association.

This distinction began to be obvious as the Sunday schools became more closely related to their own particular denominations. Some denominations aligned themselves more with the evangelical style of the Sunday School Union while others lined up with the Religious Education Association. *Some* independent publishing companies came on the scene with the major purpose of staying faithful to the older forms of the Sunday school and the more conservative theological stances. They followed the work of the American Tract Society and the American Sunday School Union.

Shortly after World War II, with the post-war baby boom and the new peacetime lifestyle, the churches that began to be called the mainline denominations all experienced a new growth of membership. Many of them reemphasized the church's evangelism mission with a new method known as "visitation evangelism." It was a program that involved training teams of two lay leaders to visit church prospects and their families to get them to promise to place membership in a local congregation. This program started almost totally outside the ministry of the church school and other educational programs of the church. Some religious education leaders rejected this approach because it focused primarily on membership recruitment and had little or no regard for the long term goals of meeting persons' need to develop spiritually after joining the church.

Also during the fifties, the leaders of many Sunday schools became more aware of the crass methods of "child evangelism" being utilized by some churches, with lessons about "little evil hearts that are going to hell" or a weekly call to "give your heart to Jesus." They intentionally began to throw out any activities or rituals that might have the same manipulative effect as contradictory to sound educational methods.

Many church school leaders felt that the old methods of the Sunday school were no longer relevant. Churches abandoned the opening exercises, attendance charts disappeared from the classroom walls, and attendance pins were discarded as old-fashioned. They also rejected many of the outlandish attendance contests, such as the one where the pastor would cut off his favorite tie if a certain goal were attained. Such antics simply stole time away from the teachers who were attempting to see that authentic learning was going on. While all this criticism may have had some valid basis, no new methods or activities replaced the old ones that would demonstrate the importance of regular attendance.

In the 1960s Christian education expanded its commitment to interdenominational partnerships in recognition of the oneness of the church and with an awareness that each denomination and its heritage could enrich the others. As new programs and curriculum resources emerged from these joint ventures, they reflected a new style of tolerance toward the beliefs and practices of each denominational family. In some cases the resulting materials or programs, in deference to a newly learned ecumenical spirit, avoided any challenge for a personal commitment or a particular faith stance lest they might appear judgmental or divisive. This tended to play down the importance of how one articulates his/her own commitment to Christ or the church because it called for an openness to all affirmations of faith.

The same spirit of "openness"—for all the appropriate reasons— also fostered a style of education that called for each person to be faithful and consistent with his/her own true feelings. On the negative side, this could mean that if one does not feel fully commited to the church, perhaps one should not *have* to attend church school. For others, it could mean that "You don't have to attend church every week to be a good Christian." Or, at least, one should not attend simply because Mom and Dad forced one, nor as a mere victim of habit, nor for seeking social status.   This style of free thinking downplayed anyone who was too overly confident in their faith commitment and discouraged anyone from making a strong witness of their faith to others lest he or she be seen as judgmental and overbearing.

Teachers were no longer trained to insist that children attend each week. Children were often not registered, their attendance not recorded, and parents were not contacted when children were absent. The quality of the teaching and implementation of more creative teaching activities were emphasized while evangelism was neglected. It left the impression that if a Sunday school lesson were good enough, children, youth, and adults would automatically want to invite new friends, and these persons could not resist the temptation to join the Sunday school.

In the 1970s a new emphasis on evangelism grew up around the research and resources of the Church Growth Movement. Much of this movement took place in churches that were evangelical descendants of the American Sunday School Union. Most mainline church educators automatically rejected the new insights of church growth research, assuming these were meant to perpetuate a style of learning that contradicted their liberal view of education. While some evangelism departments in congregations began to implement these new principles, few church educators applied them to the church school.

The Beat Goes On

Today there is still suspicion between those who feel that the church needs to recapture its evangelical mission and those who champion the importance of improving the church's educational methods.

As recently as 1984, the Disciples of Christ published *Foundational Aims of Christian Education*, which was to set their agenda for the coming decades. J. Cy Rowell authored this manual, which outlined five major aims of Christian education. It assumes that the responsibility for evangelism lies in some other ministry than that of the church school. This is apparent when Rowell states:

> Christian education is a distinct part of the work of the church, yet it is related to the total work of the church. Like evangelism and worship which enrich the life of the church through their particular concerns, Christian education exists for the church and its ministry in the world.[4]

This statement seems to imply a separation of the functions of Christian education from the functions of evangelism, even though they are actually interrelated. If such a separation is lived out, the results are apt to be a failure of the church school to incorporate outreach within its perceived responsibility, within its foundational aims.

While discussing the implications for teaching youth, noting that all persons at each age are to be biblically informed, Rowell says that "For youth, the purpose of Bible study is to enable them to "accept" the gospel story," not with a ". . .blind or forced belief; rather it means that youth need to see and hear the claims the gospel makes on their lives and to make a decision for or even against the validity of these claims."[5] This is about the only clear reference to a teaching activity that directly calls for a decision of faith or a conversion.

The whole document proceeds with the implicit assumption that the focus of the church school is to nurture and to lead into a deeper commitment of faith those who currently attend or who are members of families who attend. What seems to be lacking is the notion that another, equally important, "aim" of Christian education is to teach the conviction that each Christian is to reach out and share his or her faith with those not in the church, and to equip teachers and students alike to be able to do that reaching out.

The Division of Education and Publication of the United Church of Christ in 1986 composed a statement setting forth their intent to . . .

> develop an educational concept, a program and adequate resources based upon: (1) an understanding of how the

church is empowered to educate persons for Christian life, faith and discipleship amidst the various settings of life, including the church school. . . .[6]

This document addresses the needs and goals of Christian education for the future. Yet it seems only to plan or suggest actions that are meant for those already in the church, equipping them for the ministry of the church. There are no specific statements that would recognize the need for leaders effectively to call the unchurched into discipleship.

In 1986 the executive committee of Joint Educational Development, representing several denominations planning for a new curriculum, revised their position paper and mission statement, *A Stance Toward the Future.* This document sets the goals of the denominations in a section titled "Intentions of Educational Ministry."

The Christian community engages in a dynamic process of education as a means of sharing the gospel and inviting persons to make and live out their commitment to Christ; . . . as a means of helping persons to make their own responses of faith; to broaden and deepen their perceptions of God, the reality of sin and salvation, other persons, social issues and structures and the natural world.[7]

This statement outlines the integral relationship that exists between the ministry of Christian education and evangelism. It is hoped that this will result in JED programs and curriculum that include specific guidelines or strategies for teachers and leaders to facilitate this "inviting persons to commitment to Christ."

In 1986 two divisions of the National Council of Churches, representing the ministries of education and evangelism, convened a meeting to discuss how to find ways to overcome the gap that has developed between them at the congregational, the denominational, and the national ecumenical levels. Following this conference a study book was produced for congregational use titled *Moments of Commitment: Years of Growth.* In the book, David L. Bartlett says

The faith journey of every committed Christian has included both the gift of evangelism and the gift of Christian education. Put more broadly, each of us lives out of both nurture and decision. Each of us lives out of moments of commitment and years of growth.[8]

Most of the suggestions of this conference have implications for the local parish.

In today's dialogue about religious education, John Westerhoff has emerged as a most helpful thinker and author of new concepts for the church educator. In a recent article in *Religious Education,* he points out that there are three processes in the educational task of the church, which he calls "Catechesis": (1) *formation*—to experience Christian faith and life; (2) *education*—to reflect on the meaning of the experience of coming into Christian faith and life; and (3) *instruction*—to acquire knowledge and skills considered necessary and useful to Christian life.[9] He suggests that the step of "formation" is "an intentional process of initiation and incorporation into a Christian faith community with distinctive understandings and ways of life which differentiate it from the general culture."[10] Westerhoff believes this is a distinctive step that has been misunderstood, badly neglected, and generally mishandled by Christian education.

Another current scholar of importance to religious educators is Maria Harris. In several of her recent books she outlines a much broader understanding of the scope of the church's educational ministry than just the traditional Sunday school. While she has not criticized most church education as having neglected its evangelistic task, she has emphasized the need for personal reform or transformation. She says

... when I speak about the need to claim the power to reform as part of educational activity, I am saying that reforming is a given in life. If an organism is living and dynamic, a pattern of forming and reforming soon establishes itself. The continuing re-creation of form signals an organism's health.[11]

A Call for a Broader Definition of Christian Education

While Christian education ought to recapture its historic partnership with evangelism, let us not abandon any commitments we already feel are important. Let us restore a more balanced view of the goals of Christian education. I suggest four such goals:

The Four Goals of Christian Education

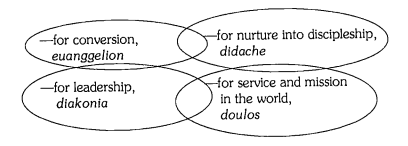

1. Education for Conversion, Transformation

This goal is: (a) to lead (educate) people to acknowledge and understand their faith; (b) to bring them (whoever they are) into the community of the faithful, the church; and (c) to encourage them to adopt the Christian lifestyle as committed disciples. This involves calling for a decision that must be appropriate for each one's own experience and age level. The Greek word *euanggelion* means proclamation of the gospel. It is a useful word to express one goal of Christian education. Proclamation through education confronts people with their own need to decide about the claims of the gospel. Such education involves providing a certain amount of information, clarifying values, and focusing on issues about the church so the candidates can decide on the validity of the gospel to their lives.

2. Education for Nurture in Discipleship

This is the traditional realm of the Sunday school. This means passing on the stories of the faith, the heritage of the church, and the values held by a particular parish. It calls for transformation in the lives of members of the faith community as they experience their own transitions in life and their own crises of faith.

The Greek word *didache* has been used to identify the "teaching" of the church—the ideas, facts, theological understanding of faith—that is passed from rabbi to disciple, from teacher to student, from preacher to laity, from generation to generation.

For Christian education that is true *nurture,* the setting must be supportive of persons, inclusive of all who call themselves Christian. The Sunday school is well equipped for this goal of education because of its traditional age level groupings, its dependence upon curriculum, and its training for teachers.

3. Education for Leadership in the Church

The Sunday school in its early days was organized in such a manner that persons who joined had a clearly visible means of learning how to assume the leadership tasks needed for the school to carry on its program. Each class, especially for adults, was organized generally around democratic structures, with clearly defined jobs for each volunteer who was elected or appointed.

The Greek word *diakonia,* meaning "servant," represents the church's need for servants to do the work of the church, its ministry to itself, and its service in the world.

Christian education must equip all members of the church to fulfill their leadership roles and tasks so that the church can carry out its ministry.

4. Education for Mission

Truly educating people of faith to carry out the mission of the church will empower them to act in the name of Christ and the church, to feed the hungry, to clothe the naked, to visit the sick, to set free those who are captive, and to serve in Christ's name all the children of God.

In recent years, the advent of the Christian Education: Shared Approaches curriculum, (especially the approach called "Doing the Word") recognized that being servants or slaves of Christ (*douloi*) often requires a transformation in each Christian's life, a conversion for persons to act for justice and peace and to organize for social change in this world.

These goals seem to follow a logical progression that parallels one's life experience in the church. However, all of these realms are at work within each Christian at the same time. Some take a more important role at one stage of our lives, while others stand out as more crucial at another. Some persons come to a deep commitment and confess a faith in the claims of the gospel because they have encountered the church by participating in some of its mission work of service to the poor. Still, most children and adults who are in the church now came to their deep personal faith through the maturing process of nurture by Christian teachers.

The main point, of course, is that we need to find ways for education to recover visibly the partnership with evangelism. As John Westerhoff has noted, "until we find a place for evangelism and conversion within our educational ministry, the church's educational mission will remain impotent."[12]

What Is Needed to Renew the Partnership?

There is a lot of work to be done to institute the changes such a new view suggests. Briefly, I would propose some ways to renew the partnership between education and evangelism.

1. *For those scholars who are defining the aims and objectives for Christian education in the next decades:*
   a. Research the historic roots in the ancient church, the church of the renaissance, the historic Sunday school movement, the new insights from faith development theory and liberation theologies in order to define an authentic role for conversion in the agenda for Christian education.
   b. Research and develop methods that are sound educationally, appropriate to each age level, and thoroughly Christian, which teachers can use to call for decisions and/or commitment from students in their Sunday school classes.

2. *For those denominational leaders who develop curriculum and supportive materials (magazines, manuals, etc.):*
   a. Recognize that some Sunday school attenders and visitors are not members of the faith community and that an important aspect of the ministry of Christian education is to proclaim the gospel to the unchurched, to invite persons to accept its claims, in a way that is appropriate to each age level. For those who identify themselves as members of the church, there is always a constant need to be reformed.
   b. Plan material for classroom teachers that gives guidance on:
      (1) ways to develop a loving, caring environment in the class;

(2) ways to reach out to the unchurched;

(3) ways to increase attendance;

(4) ways to teach pupils how to articulate their faith to others;

(5) ways to call for decisions about values and faith.

c. Provide appropriate resources in the teachers packets, such as:

(1) attendance rosters and charts to register attendance;

(2) postcards to remember birthdays, encourage absentees, and extend get well wishes;

(3) posters to encourage attendance and to set attendance goals;

(4) posters that suggest ways to articulate faith to the unchurched.

3. *For those denomination leaders who plan and conduct training for leaders in congregations and parishes:*

a. Introduce effective church growth principles to local church leaders in the ministry of Christian education.

b. Design methods to assist teachers in enabling students to articulate their faith to the unchurched and to invite the unchurched into Christian discipleship.

c. Train teachers to select learning activities and to frame questions that will call Sunday school pupils to a personal commitment that is appropriate for their stage of faith development and age.

4. *For local church leaders and administrators in the ministry of Christian education:*

a. Be alert to visitors.

b. Train parents in how to lead their children into decisions about the meaning of the gospel in the children's lives. Most training focuses on effective family relationships and not enough on how to pass on faith traditions.

c. Meet with the other evangelism or outreach boards in the congregation and plan to join strategies.

5. *For church school classroom teachers:*

a. Set a warm and loving climate in the classroom so that all students feel a strong sense of belonging.

b. Train your students to be more inclusive of visitors.

c. Extend that fellowship by teaching pupils to look outside the class for other students to invite and to care for.

d. Recognize that there are distinctions among students in your class. There are some who have been nurtured in the Christian community all their lives and who are very familiar with the major facts of our faith; others are less knowledgeable but have a strong sense of membership in the fellowship; others may not have been encouraged to commit their lives for discipleship. Each kind of student may require a different teaching style, or at least a different sensitivity from the teacher.

e. At appropriate times, and in methods that match the faith development of your class's age level, call for personal decisions or commitment to the gospel.

Conclusion

As Bartlett and Fowler have pointed out, "Christian education which nurtures discipleship will not only deepen understanding, it will ask for commitment."[13]

As the church faces the challenges of the new decade, indeed, a new century, a fundamental dichotomy between Christian education and evangelism is inappropriate. To perpetuate the controversy diverts attention and robs the church school of its energy. It is time to recapture a partnership among these two interrelated ministries in order to forge a new agenda for the promising future of Sunday school.

3

Principles for Church School Growth

"When did we see thee a stranger and welcome thee?"
—Matthew 25:38

Every congregation must do its own soul searching, and find its own way to grow.
—G.W. Garvin[1]

.For over a decade numerous denominations have been conducting research about growing congregations. They have collected impressive data that describes the characteristics common to each congregation that is growing. This chapter will report many of these characteristics and then outline which of them can be used as principles of church school growth. We hope these guidelines will help you plan for and experience growth in your church school.

The research on church growth that is most familiar has been done by such organizations as the Alban Institute of Washington, D.C., the American Institute of Church Growth, and by Lyle Schaller of the Yokefellow Institute of Richmond, Indiana.

Misconceptions About Church Growth

One significant finding has laid to rest a commonly held misunderstanding that only conservative churches are growing. When Dean Kelly wrote his popular book, *Why Conservative Churches Are Growing*, he reinforced the commonly held assumption that the only growing churches happen to be the ones that are the more evangelical and conservative. That assumption is not entirely accurate. Statistics have shown that there has been growth in the churches of conservative denominations while, for the most part, the more mainline Protestant churches have been declining. For almost all denominations, the decline in church school attendance has outstripped the decline in church membership at a rate of two to one.

Yet this assumption (that only the more evangelical churches are growing while mainline churches are declining) does not hold true for the specific congregations within each denomination. In fact, there are proportionally as many congregations within mainline churches that are growing as there are within conservative denominations. Likewise, there are as many congregations in the conservative denominations that are declining as there are in the mainline denominations.

Another misunderstanding is often used as a criticism of church growth principles by persons whose church commitment makes them strong advocates of peace and justice issues. Those persons claim that church growth, derived from these principles, produces only the kind of churches that are composed of members all from the same racial and social class. This principle of guaranteed "homogeneity" (with its potential for excluding other races, other economic classes or ethnic groups) is claimed as reason enough to reject the insights of the Church Growth Movement.

While this principle of homogeneity has proved to be useful in indigenous mission movements around the world, it is appropriate to criticize any growth strategies that exclude persons on the basis of race, age, social class, or ethnic background.

Closer examination of those churches that are growing has demonstrated that just as many of the churches that cherish diversity in age range, socio-economic class, and race are growing as are those that exhibit a more "homogeneous" makeup. Those churches that are growing may find their own unique diversity as the very quality that has the most appeal for prospective members. The churches that are more diverse have learned to live creatively with the conflicts and differences that will naturally occur between the various groups.

Many religious attitude surveys have shown that the majority of the baby boomers who are now so ready to return to church for their own moral and religious enrichment are committed to social justice and equality and are seeking a vehicle for expressing that yearning in service to others. A commitment to social justice and peace issues may be the very winsome identity that is inviting to outsiders.

Not only has research dispelled some inaccurate assumptions, it has also produced some other helpful information. This research helps us understand that there are different criteria for (a) what motivates a person to visit a church for the first or second time, (b) what motivates that same person later to choose to join the membership of a particular congregation, and, later on, (c) what motivates the person to choose to remain as an active member rather than burn out or drop out in times of difficult personal or institutional stress.[2]

These common characteristics of growing churches can also be applied as principles for planning and implementing strategies that will increase church school attendance. This chapter seeks to outline those basic principles.

There are three axioms that must be recognized before any plan for increasing church school attendance is put into practice:

- —No two congregations, regardless of how similar they might be, will grow at the same pace. What works in one situation may not work in others. There are many other intervening variables that affect growth, such as the community where it is located, age makeup of the congregation, quality of leadership, and quality of relationships within the congregation.
- —Any growth in the church school will come only as the result of a great deal of work. This means that volunteer leaders and church staff may have to reassess how best to use their time. Most of us simply cannot do more work but must give up activities that are less important for those items that are now more important to us.
- —In order for church leaders to accept the new responsibilities, they will need to overcome an unconscious fear of change and to alter their assumption that growth is very unlikely.

Principles for the Growth of the Church School

1. The Church School Will Grow Whose Members Believe That Growth Is Possible and Appropriate.

The most important ingredient that determines whether or not any congregation will grow is its basic attitude. Most churches can experience growth if members simply create a well thought-out plan and work diligently to carry out that plan. Herb Miller of the Christian Church (Disciples of Christ) has said:

> Mainline congregations must answer six basic questions . . . to determine if they are really motivated to compete for non-church members: Do they want, seek, invite, welcome, involve and nurture company?[3]

2. The Church School Will Grow in the Congregation That Places High Value on Christian Education.

Are there adequate financial resources spent for curriculum, equipment, resources, teacher training, youth programming, and elective programs for adults? Does the minister participate in the planning and goal setting for the ministry of Christian education? Does the pastor teach on a regular basis? Is there a regular process for advertising the programs of Christian education throughout the entire congregation? Are parents and students generally satisfied with their church school experience and are they willing to speak positively about it to others in and outside the church? Do adults regularly participate in events that are designed for their own Christian education or do they assume that Sunday school is just for kids? Does the whole church celebrate achievements and transitions of persons involved in the education programs of the church? The answers to these questions will give a good picture of how well the congregation supports Christian education.

Sometimes the church school leaders have worked so hard for so long that they experience burnout and can no longer generate the enthusiasm for education within the whole church. A defeated leadership and an apathetic congregation make church school growth almost impossible. This book provides some handles so a new spirit of joy and enthusiasm can restore the sense of importance that Christian education must play in the church.

3. The Church School Will Grow Whose Members Are Able to Say Who They Are, in a Winsome and Inviting Manner.

In order for members of the church school, as well as teachers and leaders, to be effective at inviting prospective visitors they must be able to describe what makes their church a special and welcome place to be. Often this is spoken in the language of friendship. "The members of my church are the friendliest people I have ever met," someone will say. Others can refer to an exciting and comprehensive program. Still others might say that they have really been challenged to a stronger faith or to greater service in Christ's name.

Usually it is the newest members who are best able to say why they like your church, because they have so recently made their decision to become members and can clearly recall their reasons for doing so. They are often the best ambassadors for inviting visitors.

Another method of identifying the winning qualities of any church is to ask the members, "Why do you attend this church rather than some other?" For many of the growing churches this identity includes a strong commitment in time and stewardship to the local community and worldwide mission of the church.

The curriculum materials that have been produced in most denominations over the recent decades have given little guidance to teachers in how to train pupils to speak to persons outside the church about why the Christian faith and church membership are important to them. This responsibility for training church members in how and why to share their faith is very important for the growth of the Christian faith as well as for increasing the membership of the church school.

The following questions might be used to help adults learn how to talk about what faith means to them in a winning way.

1. How old were you or what was happening in your life when you remember being able to call yourself a Christian for the first time?
2. What is the most important quality about your church?
3. What person or church leader in your life had the most influence on what your church life or faith means to you today? Why was that person so important?
4. What were your most memorable feelings that you can recall when you first began coming to this church?

5. At what time of personal transition or crisis was the church (or friends in the church) most helpful to you?

4.The Church School Will Grow That Helps Persons to Feel That They Belong and Their Presence Is Prized.

It is a basic principle of learning theory that students learn best where they feel love and acceptance. A feeling of belonging is necessary for the consistent attendance needed for progressive learning that builds on ideas and facts learned earlier. Recent research has demonstrated that people are looking for a church that is loving and caring. Dr. Win Arn of the Institute for American Church Growth recently reported that most churches that are growing have learned how to love, according to a survey he conducted of church members respresenting thirty-nine denominations. This research has shown a connection between a denomination's "love ability" and its membership growth or decline.[4] This suggests that one of the most significant responsibilities of every teacher is to make each pupil feel welcome and cherished.

One congregation has encouraged each church school teacher to spend some time in each class session to ask the pupils to identify those who are absent. Then a suggestion is made about how that person might be contacted.

5. The Church School Will Grow That Seeks New Members Through the Friendship and Kinship Ties of Current Members.

Interviews with new church members have demonstrated that most people (77.6 percent) attend church for the first time because other persons have invited them or because they are connected through family ties to other members of the church.[5] Only a very small percentage indicate that they had attended several churches when looking for a new church.

Of course, many new members of the church school are born into the families that are already members, which produces a kind of biological growth. Others come through the invitation of a cousin, a brother- or sister-in-law, or even a spouse.

It is common for children to bring their best friends to vacation church school or to a class party. Adults usually invite a new neighbor who has moved in near them, a colleague at work, someone they play bridge with, or someone they know through other networks of friends.

A basic principle for increasing a list of prospects for the church is to ask the newest members of the church to identify those friends, family members, neighbors, or casual acquaintances who have not already been involved in the church. Almost always names will emerge that would be very good prospects.

Then the church school can devise some way to extend an invitation to those persons. Among that list of contacts is another set of persons that can identify further contacts. This process is described as always working to the outside of the network. What is the network? It is that complex mixture of lists of persons. Within the network there is one person who also knows some of the people you know and a lot of people you have not met. Those who are strangers to you know many other persons, and so the network extends on and on.

6. The Church School Will Grow That Takes Seriously the Spiritual Growth and Personal Life Concerns of All People.

"[People] are seeking a church that can respond effectively to the needs they encounter on their personal and spiritual journey in life. This often means the church with a strong evangelistic thrust must strengthen its adult ministries."[6] You must ask the question: What issue in people's lives do they feel most concerned about? This question is much different from the one that asks: What do I think these people need to know or learn? The former question requires a sympathetic style of thinking and not one based on your church's need to grow. This perspective is a more truly caring attitude.

The courses, the classes, the educational opportunities must take seriously that people are asking faith questions of the events of their lives. It is well known that people are most open to ask questions of faith and morals at times of great transitions in their lives. That is why people who have recently been unemployed, divorced, relocated or retired, or have recently seen their youngest child go off to college, are the best prospects for a church school class or program and for joining the church. Sometimes small groups of persons who are struggling with the same life concerns can be brought together in a study or support group to help them find a common bonding and a faith dimension to their struggle.

The church school must also reach out to the neighborhood where it is located. When you do that regularly, demonstrating honest interest in the people's life struggles, the community will take your advertising more seriously. The church school program can show that you care for the persons in the community.

7. The Church School Will Grow That Has Easy Access for Newcomers and a Welcoming Environment.

In most church buildings a visitor or newcomer can be very confused about where to find the appropriate classroom. This is especially true of buildings that were constructed in several different stages. In some places one cannot find a place to park. Then, when one starts to go in the nearest door, she or he finds it is locked (probably because it goes into a boiler room, or it is used by the children in a weekday preschool to get to the playground). Every church must do all it can to reduce the number of ways a newcomer can be discouraged by such blocks.

To help a church school grow, great care must be taken to show newcomers where to enter the church, how to find a nursery, how to make a decision about the proper class for their interests and needs, and how to find that class. For most buildings, adequate signs, conveniently located maps, and well-lit entrances and hallways can overcome most confusing architectural barriers. In others, the problem can only be solved with live persons who serve as greeters and guides. These greeters can also make records of names and addresses and other pertinent information.

Only recently have we become sensitized to the barriers most buildings present to handicapped persons. Those churches are growing that help persons in wheelchairs reach classrooms and the sanctuary. Adequate ramps and elevators are needed for each floor. Other handicaps, such as sight or hearing impairment, need attention as well.

Besides a sense of easy access or entrance into the church, a newcomer is greatly influenced by the way the building is kept clean and repaired. A church that is dirty and needs repair speaks loudly to say, "The members here do not care much about this church."

Adults who visit a church school classroom for the first time will be embarrassed as they enter if the persons already there ignore them and if no one helps them find a seat. This can easily happen if a newcomer is late and class members fear a commotion will disrupt the teacher. Sometimes it can be a help to see that the class does not face the entrance to the classroom so that if a visitor arrives late it is easier to find a seat without feeling as if the entire class is staring at the one who causes the interruption. If the teacher faces the door and the pupils face away, the teacher can more easily handle the disruption so that visitors feel more welcome and less an intrusion.

When members have attended a particular church for a long time, they forget how it feels to be a stranger. So, to get a better idea of the first impression we present, it is good practice to ask newcomers what they noticed when they first visited your church. It also helps to take notes of your first impressions anytime you enter a new building for the first time—bank, school, office, museum, fast food restaurant. Just notice what aids help you find your way around. What colors and decor make you feel comfortable? What employee behavior helps you feel at ease and welcome?

The church school whose members want it to grow must be a place of welcome. We are reminded of Jesus' parable of the judgment, in which people say, "Lord, when did we see you a stranger and welcome you?"

8. The Church School Will Grow That Provides Quality Programs.

Today's consumer society assumes that it has the right to expect quality programs. Most adults are substantially better educated than previous generations. They see outstanding leadership in the television and media. They send their children to the best schools and they have readily available the broadest selection of consumer products. They expect to be able to demand the best quality in whatever they choose.

Because of this attitude, the church school will grow only if it demonstrates that it takes its job seriously. Parents will look for programs and teachers that their children enjoy and find challenging. Those adults will also expect quality programs for themselves. Such programs must meet real personal and family needs.

To meet the varieties of appetites of the different ages and stages of adult development, there needs to be a variety in the teaching methods and topics. It is equally important that teaching methods, curriculum materials, and media resources be appropriate to the age-level needs of all children and youth.

9. The Church School Will Grow That Is Able to Open Up New Entrances into the Church While Reducing the Number of Exits.

Probably no single step will increase attendance in Sunday school as much as a conscientious effort to prevent members from dropping out. It is essential for a teacher to notice whenever there is a change in attendance pattern in some class member. When someone is absent, a teacher or leader might assume that there is a simple explanation and that the member will resume regular attendance soon. Then, if the teacher forgets to follow up, the individual may become totally inactive.

Any effort to keep all members active will pay off in attendance growth. If the church school leaders paid more attention to such changes in the attendance patterns, they might give real ministry where it is needed and soon restore the dropouts to full participation. Once a member has dropped out over several months, the chances of a return are greatly reduced.

It must be noted that the practical application of this principle is that clear and accurate attendance records are absolutely necessary to follow the members and to monitor their attendance patterns in order to prevent dropout. Such records are also required to develop a prospect list from the names of visitors and persons who could be candidates for new classes and new programs.

The best entrance into active participation for many prospects is through some small group in the church. It could be a church school class, a choir, or some special support group. .

The church school is the best organized system in the church to establish new classes and groups that will meet the needs of newcomers. It must be fully prepared for new classes before the prospects are recruited. Too often we think, "If a group wants a new class we will be glad to start it." Yet this attitude requires the initiative to come from the prospect or newcomer. Newcomers have neither the ability nor the experience to plan and initiate new classes or groups in the church.

10. The Church School Will Grow That Can Welcome New Members and Assimilate Them into the Leadership of the Church.

Because some churches have stayed the same size for so many years, they do not expect to grow. In fact, they may even unconsciously resist the influx of too many new members because it could substantially change the character of the church life they cherish. While few church members could honestly admit to themselves that they might resent such growth, there is still more resistance than we generally acknowledge. This most often appears as a resistance to change rather than a resistance to visitors or newcomers.

Newcomers can experience this resistance when they feel left out of all the life stories shared in a Sunday school class. These stories are often repeated at fellowship and social times. Care must be taken to hear the stories of the newcomer. The class must also help newcomers to learn the heritage of the group they are entering.

Plans should also be made to reduce the time a person has to be a member before feeling free to contribute to the group life. One less threatening way to overcome this resistance to newcomers is to start new classes in which all members of a new group share in a fresh start.

Another indicator of whether newcomers are welcome is the length of time it takes for them to have a chance to assume a major role in the leadership and decision–making processes of the group. One hint about how easily a newcomer is accepted as a leader is the way her or his suggestions and ideas are handled. There must be a real desire to hear the fresh insights from newcomers. Likewise, they must receive help or gentle counsel to adapt their ideas to the present group.

The worst thing that occurs in some churches is giving newcomers important jobs when they are too inexperienced to be able to do the jobs well. This is especially sad when longtime members believe there is only one way the job should be done. If the new volunteer is not assisted with advice and counsel then he or she could very easily become embarrassed, get burned-out, and give up. When this has happened and the new leader drops out, the old-timers usually conclude that the person was simply not "committed" enough in the first place. Then the old-timers resist giving leadership responsibility to the next newcomer.

These *ten basic principles of church school growth* are tools to help churches plan their course of action. They can be used as guidelines to choose where to begin and what to do next. As principles they can serve like rulers to measure whether or not the ideas are likely to be productive. Once a church catches the vision of a new life and adopts an optimistic and enthusiastic attitude, all kinds of new ideas begin to emerge. For the best results, each suggestion, each idea needs to fit into a total plan. These ten church school growth principles can be used as tools to help choose which plans are best for one's church.

After all is said and done, every church must ask itself the more important question, "Will this idea really work in our church?" If not, "How should it be different in our situation?" Any guidelines or principles that are half-heartedly applied because some *expert* suggested them are not likely to produce the desired results. On the other hand, any principle that is adjusted and then enthusiastically adopted because it makes sense, is bound to produce greater results.

Fifteen Practical Steps to Begin Increasing Church School Attendance

The following are some specific recommendations that can be done right away to bring about some progress. They can help even before the entire congregation learns how to change its attitudes and behaviors. They can be adopted and put into place as a way of helping the church see that there truly are some things that can be done. A person can start to work on any one or all of these practical hints almost immediately.

It remains true that some may be productive in one church while others will not. The success or failure of any of these helpful steps hinges on the climate of the congregation—on the extent to which the basic principles listed above are already unconsciously a part of that parish's common attitudes and program.

   1. *Set goals for higher attendance.* The exercise of setting realistic goals for higher attendance will raise everyone's consciousness about the importance of working on increasing attendance. At first be sure the goals are gradual and attainable. One caution about attendance contests is in order: Most contests of an earlier era focused on recruiting first-time attenders and did not include some method by which to continue to nurture these newcomers in order for them to become full-time members.

2. *Keep accurate and comprehensive attendance records.* This is a task that is most often the responsibility of the classroom teacher or adult class officer. Immediate follow-up on visitors and regular recognition for birthdays, anniversaries, sickness, divorce, promotions, or other achievements or misfortunes of the members are great attendance builders. They especially build loyalty. It cannot be said too clearly that this is a major responsibility for any teacher.

3. *Develop lists of prospects.* The names and addresses of visitors and newcomers must be conscientiously recorded. Some churches have found that the commercial computer software is a great help in this process. This list is then used to advertise any program of the church school. Names of prospects can come from those who have visited, from friends of members, from direct mailing lists of residents who live near the church, from persons who send children to your day care or preschool programs, from persons who attend your Christmas Eve service, from couples who come to find a church in which to be married.

   Those who work hard at maintaining accurate lists of names for prospects are often amazed at how quickly the list can grow to immense proportions.

   Keep in mind that some prospects take several months, even a couple of years, before they really become candidates for church membership in your parish. Do not become too easily discouraged.

   Long-time members of the church who are not already members of the church school are not good prospects for this list. They have already made their decision about whether or not they want to be involved in Christian education.

4. *Use newcomers to help tell the story of the joy, the excitement, the value, and the faith that is available in your church school.* They are usually more able to say specifically why they chose to join your church school, so they are your best ambassadors.

5. *Train members how to invite their friends and their acquaintances to join them at church.* Sometimes it has not even occurred to children to ask their friends to come along

to church. Adults usually need help to overcome their self-consciousness. They can be shown to invite their friends to come along to special celebrations or parties as a first step.

6.   *Have greeters at each entrance of the church* (a) to meet newcomers, (b) to get their names, and (c) to show them the way to find their proper classrooms. Use children and youth as well as adults for greeters.

7.   *Have immediate follow-up visits or telephone contacts with all visitors.* This is best done by the laity and not by paid professional church staff. Some research has shown that personal contact of visitors within thirty-six hours of their visit will produce an 85 percent return rate. The longer time that lapses between the visit and the church's contact reduces the likelihood of the visitor returning. It drops to 60 percent after seventy-two hours.[7]

8.   *Use name tags often to help church members get acquainted with any new visitors.*   ·

9.   *Start new classes.* Expand the choices of learning methods for adults. Take into account the special ways each age level prefers to learn.

10.   *Have leaders and teachers prepared before you begin a new class.* Do not start such a new venture by simply asking people to attend a set-up meeting if you are not absolutely positive that you can offer that new class or program.

11.   *Reduce physical barriers for persons who are handicapped.*

12.   *Use lots of clear directional signs,* both for entrances into the church and also for directions within the church.

13.   *Provide ample parking.* Designate some spaces for first-time visitors only.

14.   *Reach out by advertising the church school programs*

within the church. The entire church will be more enthusiastic about inviting newcomers to church school if they can see the numerous programs that are available for them. Celebrating your successes with the whole church has great public-relations value.

15. *Advertise within the community.* Remember a good rule for public relations by directing your advertising to the felt needs of those who hear and read it rather than sharing what you feel people "ought" to know.

Here are fifteen helpful hints. Choose a few to begin working on this year. These practical steps for increasing church school attendance may apply just as well to all the other programs of the church. They also show the way in which the church's ministry of nurture, evangelism, and service all depend upon each other in order for growth to occur.

The church school can and does provide an education in a unique setting and with a caring style that meets personal needs in a way that no other institution in our society does. We can be proud of the mandate of Christ. We truly can and must make strangers into neighbors, visitors into friends.

4

Roadblocks, Detours, and Barriers

. . . let us also lay aside every weight, and sin which clings so closely, and let us run with perseverance the race that is set before us.

—Hebrews12:1

There is no easy answer or surefire prescription for church school growth. . . .Probably any church school can grow if it really wants to grow.

—Kenneth D. Blazier[1]

Have you heard yourself complain that you wished people in your congregation were just a little more enthusiastic or more committed to the work of the church? Most church school leaders tend to be discouraged about the current conditions in their churches. In many congregations the Sunday school attendance has been declining for as many as thirty years. The leaders of such congregations have gotten into the habit of not expecting any growth in their church school. It is as if they have become programmed to expect failure.

Why is the present situation so discouraging? When we ask that question, we usually hear a long list of adjectives that describe the people in our church, blaming them for our current condition. We say they are apathetic, not committed, bored, burned-out, lazy, set in their old ways, unenthusiastic. While these labels reveal our frustration with other people's attitudes, they do not help us to get on with the business of the church.

Some may blame themselves for not trying hard enough. Other people may blame the pastor or some other church leaders as the cause for the decline. Still others blame the curriculum materials or any other number of perceived causes. There is no single cause, but a complex set of various influences on attendance in the church school.

Some other causes have been mentioned in earlier chapters, such as the fact that the birthrate was very low between 1968 and 1976. For that reason there are simply fewer children and youth in the population now than previously. Another reason for the decline is that between 1960 and 1980 many in our society rejected membership in all institutions, including the church. We have no reason to blame ourselves for these circumstances, and there probably is no way we could have made them any less influential on the prevailing decline. Simply finding causes may not suggest proper solutions. Most important of all, blaming is a nonproductive solution.

One solution to the current decline may be as simple as overcoming our discouragement.

It could be that we are immobilized by our attitudes and our misconceptions. We may be apathetic because we have drawn certain conclusions about the church that are based upon ideas that are untrue. Clearer information can help overcome our discouragement.

The purpose of this chapter is to overcome some of those unhealthy attitudes and correct those bits of misinformation so that we can change our way of thinking, can be helped with some fresh suggestions, and can gain some renewed enthusiasm for our work.

Roadblocks to Growth

There are some commonly held notions that can truly be labeled as roadblocks. When they cloud our understanding, these blocks affect our thinking so much that they hinder our work. Even though they are untrue, because we believe them to be true they control our behavior and direct our decision-making. In their own powerful way they become self-fulfilling prophecies. They get in the way of our helping the church school to grow.

Let us review some of these roadblocks so they can be discarded and their power to immobilize us can be reduced.

Roadblock #1: *There are numerous prospects for the church school in our current church membership.* The truth is that current church members who are not already members of the church school are usually very poor prospects. These active members of the church who are not in the church school have already made their own decision about whether or not their interests and needs are met by the current adult classes.

Organizing new classes is the most productive way to involve these members. Otherwise, the best prospects come from outside the church school and are those visitors and friends of current members outside the church.

Roadblock #2: *Our community is not growing; there are no new families moving in so there are virtually no new prospects for our church school.* The truth is less than 5 percent of the communities in America have experienced the kind of population decline that would virtually eliminate any hope of new prospects. Instead, the best prospects are most likely to come from friends and acquaintances of members and not just from newcomers moving into a community. Many friends who are not now in the church school are new prospects when they have gone through some major transition in their lives.

Growing church schools are found in virtually any kind of community in this country, including those with changing or even declining populations.

Roadblock #3: *Why are we so concerned about just numbers? Isn't quality more important than quantity anyway?* Could it be that if we choose only "quality," we are choosing (however unintentionally) not to reach out to all those persons who have never been confronted with the claims of the gospel? We do not have to choose one or the other. In fact, church school growth requires a strong commitment to quality educational methods and programs in order for an increase in quantity of new persons to have a lasting effect. Just as important, we cannot neglect our responsibility to reach out to the unchurched.

Roadblock #4: *If our church would just get back to the basics—spend more time in just teaching the Bible—we could grow like the other churches.* This roadblock is a corollary to the assumption we dealt with in the third chapter of this book, namely, it is only the conservative churches that are growing. It is true that people are yearning for more spiritual insight into the meaning of their lives, and the Bible is the greatest source for bringing that meaning. Yet it is not true that only those churches that give great attention to Bible study and little attention to the wider mission of the church are the ones that are growing.

In some ways, this kind of thinking is merely a way of comparing today's church life with what we experienced in the 1950s when it appeared that everyone wanted to join the church. Some people feel that there was more Bible content in the curricula of that time. Yet the underlying assumption that it was more true to the Bible is unfounded. The Bible content today is still a vibrant part of the curriculum, but the style of teaching or the methods used have changed significantly.

Bob Gribbon of the Alban Institute has pointed out that any church that seeks to invite the current generation of "baby boomers" must have a clear focus on the spiritual dimensions of life:

> First and foremost, however, churches need to be attentive to their religious identity. It is not only conservative churches that are growing, but we found that baby-boomers were most responsive to those congregations which had clarity about their central religious function—people don't come primarily for the program, but for some connection with the transcendent.[2]

There are a lot more tangible factors that affect the church's growth than any particular theological stance, even though it may appear to be more popular.

Roadblock #5: *People are just not interested in the church anymore.* All the recent surveys of America's religious attitudes have shown a dramatic rise in personal faith throughout our population. In fact, one survey of teenagers (the group most often seen as the skeptics in our society) has shown that over 95 percent have a strong belief in a personal God; 70 percent pray to God; 40 percent pray on a regular basis; and half have a strong desire to serve humanity, to make this world a better place in which to live.[3]

This appetite for religious meaning in people's lives may not automatically translate into regular church school attendance. But it does mean people are more open to respond to an invitation to attend church than at any time in recent history.

Roadblock #6: *We cannot expect our church to grow because we are located in a neighborhood or community that is mostly* _____. Different people use different words to fill this blank. It is often completed with words like "old people" or some ethnic group or some other religious faith group such as "Southern Baptist," "Lutheran," or "Roman Catholic." It assumes that the neighborhood is the greatest source for prospects and that there are not likely to be any possible or desirable candidates from that particular neighborhood.

This kind of thinking arises out of the time period between 1930 and 1955 when most people who attended any congregation lived close enough to walk to church. Today nearly all pastors can tell you that only 20 to 30 percent of their church membership lives within a mile of their church building. Most people drive their cars to church, no matter how far it is.

This kind of thinking may also come from the time period when most people chose to attend a parish of the denomination in which they were raised. This is not so much the case today. Most congregations have 65 percent of their membership who grew up, or were baptized or confirmed, in some denomination other than the one they are currently attending. The overwhelming majority of first-time visitors to any church come by the invitation of a friend or acquaintance. Very few indicate that they located the church of their denominational preference upon moving into a new community.

Neighborhood location of any particular congregation is a barrier to newcomers *only* when those current church members believe it needs to be.

Roadblock #7: *Most people in our society just do not have any time for church anymore. They are too busy.* This sentiment is repeated in the lament that many mothers are employed outside the home and want to sleep in on Sunday mornings. We hear complaints that many athletic teams schedule their practices or games on Sunday. Other people suggest that people spend too much leisure time at their lake houses or with hobbies because they can now afford such luxuries. They forget about the important things of life, such as the church.

It is true that there seems to be much more competition for people's time; yet if we reflect on experience we clearly know that people choose to do what is important in their lives. There are numerous reports that many more adults each year are donating greater amounts of time as volunteers for not-for-profit agencies. Religious attitude surveys suggest that people are more concerned with faith issues in their lives and are seeking to learn more.

Detours to Growth

The preceding statements or *roadblocks* are basically untrue. We have tried to correct that misinformation because they can prevent church school growth in a powerful way. Now let us consider some other prevailing attitudes or mindsets to examine how they *detour* our efforts to grow.

The following *detours* have a lot of appeal because there is a grain of truth in what they say. Yet they are given so much credence that we are inclined to say "If that is the case, there is little or nothing that we can do about our stagnant situation."

We have heard these excuses repeated so often that we can readily sense their power to detour our attention and sap our energy. In some cases these detours are merely "lame excuses" to cover up our inaction. So "Let us throw off every weight that so easily slows us down and let us run with perseverance the race that is set before us" (Hebrews 12:1, paraphrased).

Detour #1: *We must have more young couples to join our church or we are going to die.* The corollary to this statement is that every good church must have an active youth group; if it doesn't ,then it must not be a good church.

Both of these mindsets seem to assume that middle or older adults are not desirable prospects for evangelism and are not likely to help the church school grow. (One can easily see how this even smacks of hidden ageism.) People think of a church school's membership as a progression of young couples who rear their children in the church, then progress through their lives in the church to maturity and death. This assumes that the only source of new members must be with a new, younger generation. This need not be true. It usually takes young couples to invite other young couples; yet, conversely, older adults are just as capable of bringing in newcomers as any other generation.

There is another reason why this detour has such compelling power. It focuses on a weakness of a particular congregation.While we feel guilty or inadequate about our weaknesses, guilt is not a very energizing motive. Church school growth is most apt to come when we focus on our own strengths rather than our lack of a particular program. People are attracted to our current identity—who we are—not to what we wish we were.

Detour #2: *We just can't take on any more work. We are all overworked as it is.* Sometimes this mind set is also expressed as: "We just can't stand to attend any more meetings." This kind of discouragement is a symptom of burnout and hopelessness. People will respond and give time and leadership to any project that they feel is likely to bring the hoped-for results. But they are too tired to add more responsiblity if they believe there are not apt to be any new successes.

The truth of the matter is that for any church school to begin to grow it has to reassess its priorities, to look at itself with new eyes, and to begin operating in new ways. These new ways usually mean that in order to do an effective job, leaders will have to give up some old responsibilities (especially those that have outlived their usefulness) for new tasks that are more likely to produce positive results.

Sometimes it is hard for church school leaders to realize that growth usually comes in a snowball effect. At first the progress seems hopelessly slow. Significant growth only becomes visible after a great deal of groundwork has been laid, after a few new members begin to multiply the number of new prospects that are available to visit your church school. Be easy on yourself until the multiplying effect of growth has a large enough impact for the rest of the church to be aware of the progress being made.

Detour #3: *Why are we so concerned about outsiders? We have many inactives who used to be part of this church, and now nobody seems to care a thing about them.* This is a very compelling comment because it places us in a very awkward position. It seems that there is no way we can answer this question without appearing to be uncaring persons. The choice is not simply to forget our inactives if we pursue new members. Those are two entirely different issues that require two entirely different approaches. No church need choose between the two but should be organized to do both. Generally, the church school is best equipped to concentrate on re-cruiting new members; it is not so well-equipped to revitalize inactives.

Detour #4: *We never did it that way before.* How often that kind of phrase has stifled progress in many realms of the church! Some cynic has called that phrase the "seven last words of the church."

Let us not be too flippant in trying to deal with this comment. One of the greatest barriers to church school growth is an unconscious fear of the changes that might come with the influx of too many new members too quickly. New members have new attitudes, new ideas, new and different desires and goals for the church.

Any church school that hopes to grow must be prepared to help its members learn how to embrace changes graciously and to celebrate new members.

Detour #5: *We tried it once and it didn't work.* The church is littered with new programs that promised great results but were poorly applied and too quickly abandoned. We have a tendency to enter any new activity that is recommended half-heartedly. Or we radically change the recommended methods so that they lose their power. Or we give up too soon because new leaders in the church do not see the value of the program initiated by their predecessors.

Even if the new suggestions for increasing church school attendance were used before with little results, the truth of the matter is, this is a new decade. There are new and better insights to help us avoid failure. The climate for growth is better than it has been in three decades. Having tried it once before is a poor reason for not trying again.

Detour #6: *We have always had an open door for new members. Our motto is "Everyone Is Welcome in Our Church."* It does take an open heart to make visitors feel welcome and at home, but we cannot simply stop with that feeling. We must actively invite new members into the church school. If we leave all the initiative to the prospective member to search out our location and decide when and whether to come, we will continue to decline as we have before.

Sometimes there is a bit of self-righteousness about our openness. This can become resentment over the fact that people do not seek out our church and quickly join us. Some have even said, "If these people are really serious about the church, they will come back and give us a second chance. If they are not going to be that committed, I guess we don't need that kind of church member anyway."

When we are passive in our approach to the newcomer, we are failing to be effective educators. The teacher must set the climate of excitement and acceptance in order for the student to be able to learn well. A good teacher must take more initiative in recruiting the students.

Detour #7: *I'm just too shy; I can't talk with strangers. Or, I have not been a member of this denomination long enough. Don't expect me to be a very good representative.* Many people have fears about what is expected of them as evangelists. They have unfounded assumptions that they are being asked to don burlap robes and sandals, carry signs, and preach from the street corners. Others fear they are expected to be hard-sell salespersons trying to convert the innocent and the resistant.

True evangelism for today is a matter of showing personal, caring concern for others. It means being willing to tell our own story of what is meaningful and important in our lives. Any Sunday school teacher knows that he or she never has all the answers to the questions that are likely to emerge in the classroom. We only need to be willing to explore together. Each person has a faith adequate enough to help others along on their own pilgrimages to greater faith. In most cases people are not looking for *our* answers to their problems but are looking for acceptance and help to find *their own* answers. Such enabling is the most effective teaching style as well as being the most effective evangelistic method.

Our habits of thinking tend to prevent us from working to our fullest capacity. These *roadblocks* and *detours* make church school growth difficult because they keep leaders from doing their very best.

Barriers to Growth

On the other hand, there are some real *barriers* that act as blocks to any prospective newcomers. The earlier roadblocks and detours are really hindrances to us as leaders. The following barriers are hindrances to those who visit our church and who consider becoming members of our church school.

We are rarely aware of the power these barriers exert and the negative impressions they make on visitors or new members. Some are physical barriers. Some barriers are caused by the quality of leadership and the climate of personal relationships in the church. Let us examine a few of these barriers and become more aware of their power to prevent an increase in church school attendance.

Physical Barriers

Barrier #1: *Poor Building Conditions.* When there are too many stairs to climb to enter the building or the sanctuary, when the lighting in the hallways and classrooms is dim, when the walls need several coats of paint, or when all the furniture seems sorely out-of-date and in disrepair, newcomers are wary. For some locations in the country the lack of air-conditioning in the summer is also a barrier.

Barrier #2: *Poor Location.* This barrier can be overcome by more adequate advertising. The yellow pages of the telephone directory may aid in reaching new people who move into your community. Better signs may help locate parking and entrances to the church. In some neighborhoods directional signs with arrows placed on nearby streets can help. Some congregations have found media advertising and mass mailings to the neighborhood to be of some use. However, such mailings require a rather costly outlay with very slow, long-term results.

Some Sunday schools have found that special ministries—such as programs for singles or young adults—get responses when notices are placed in the classified ads under "personal messages."

In the 1950s the congregation that found itself in a poor location was told to move the congregation, build a new facility, and begin again. This is not as valuable a suggestion as it once was. Such a move often produces a new congregation with a substantially different lifestyle from the former one. There is great wisdom in focusing on the best qualities of your current ministry rather than trying to change into a substantially different congregation.

Barrier #3: *Inadequate Parking.* This barrier is sometimes overrated for its effect on church school growth. However, our own parking situation can be improved rather easily if members of the church are trained to leave a few spaces close to the church for anyone who might be a visitor.

Barrier #4: *Barriers for Persons with Handicapping Conditions.* Our society has recently been made aware of these barriers. However, there does not always need to be major remodeling in order to remove the barriers to persons who are handicapped. Sometimes better lighting, better sound systems, carpet on entrances, or moving some classes into different classrooms can be simple solutions to the most immediate problems. It does take leaders who can look at their barriers with a new eye in order to soften or remove their effect.

Relationship Barriers

Barrier #5: *Internal Conflicts.* When visitors enter a church school class or a congregation in which there are petty jealousies, competition for power and control, or personality conflicts among members, they will think twice before wanting to enter such a group.

Often the signals of such conflicts are not very apparent. Visitors may not be able to say why the climate in any particular church school seems cool and unwelcoming, but they unconsciously sense a barrier they may choose not to cross.

Barrier #6: *Closed Cliques.* Everyone has experienced this kind of barrier in some group she or he has visited or tried to join. Leaders in the church school, however, will not solve the problem by attacking or critizing such cliques. Such close friendship ties play an important role in people's lives. Those within such a closed circle are usually not aware of the ways they shut others out, and they find that network to be a comfort and a support to their lives of faith.

Barrier #7: *Leaders with Long Tenure.* This becomes a relational barrier when the leaders of a particular group are the same persons for too long a time. At other times newcomers may be easily accepted into a church school, but they are discouraged from taking over the leadership roles because current leaders resist sharing their authority and power. This is particularly a problem in the current decade when so many of the church school's leaders have had to hold their jobs for so long because of the previous pattern of declining membership. In addition, medical advances allow older persons to stay healthy and productive longer than ever before.

Barrier #8: *Burned-out Leaders.* Leaders in the church school or teachers in the classrooms may become discouraged and begin to display other signs of "burnout." This discouragement can be quickly sensed by newcomers, and it becomes a barrier to their interest. When newcomers are given tasks in the church school with little training and no sense of the importance of their jobs, they will perpetuate the discouragement that burned-out leaders have demonstrated before. Apathy begets apathy. On the other hand, optimism and enthusiasm grow out of a sense of achievement brought about by competence and training.

Barrier #9: *Conservative Stewardship.* When a church refuses to spend adequate resources on its facilities, its curriculum, media resources, and programs, the results soon begin to show. Generous stewardship of financial resources demonstrates to visitors that something important to the lives of the members of this church is being pursued with commitment and energy.

When this stewardship includes money and personal energy given to outreach by the congregation, it becomes an encouragement to visitors and newcomers. Parents usually want their children to be taught this kind of caring and generous lifestyle.

Conclusion

It may seem difficult to solve all the problems that were introduced by this chapter on *roadblocks, detours,* and *barriers.* Any church school that wants to increase its attendance needs to be aware of these hindrances. Often identifying the demons in our lives is the strongest step toward eliminating their effect.

Changing persons' attitudes and their subsequent behaviors can be a long process. As leaders we are usually impatient about letting such a process take its proper course. We want to be able to tell the members of our church school a new fact and then expect them to begin to behave in a new and different way. We must be patient but persistent.

There is hope! We may be immobilized by our current attitudes and assumptions, yet we can be confident that clearer information can help overcome our discouragement and apathy. More accurate facts can open up new interests and give us new energy. Let us break through the roadblocks, the detours, the myths and mindsets, and let us overcome the barriers so that the church school can grow as it is designed to do.

5

Infants and Preschool Children

"And whoever welcomes in my name one such child as this, welcomes me. If anyone should cause one of these little ones to lose his faith in me, it would be better for that person to have a large millstone tied around his neck and be drowned in the deep sea."

—Matthew 18:5-6, TEV

We reach and care for all people because we believe that God cares for all regardless of age.

—Linda Chenoweth

It is possible to increase the church school attendance of young children even though we realize that most are brought to church by someone else. Infants and toddlers do not usually make their own decisions about whether or not to attend Sunday school, but if they are comfortable and seem to enjoy themselves, their parents will feel positive toward the Sunday school. If they always cry when left, or, as older children, argue about attending, parents tend to question whether or not they should insist on Sunday school. Parents or other caregivers decide whether or not to bring their children, not only because of the quality of the experience for their children, but also because of their own personal experience in the church. So, as we discuss young children in the church school we must also be planning for the parents.

For the purposes of this chapter and for a better understanding of the young child, remember that young children mature and change at such a rapid rate that there could be three or four different chapters on this topic. So we will separate the discussion about infants and toddlers (birth to two years of age) from that of the older preschool age children (two years through kindergarten).

Today's parents are looking for help in teaching their children the basic moral and religious values that are important for their children to cope and excel in the world. When parents become more acutely aware of this yearning, they may start bringing their child to the church and place it in the nursery. This coming back to church traditionally occurs when the first child is about to enter kindergarten or when a second child comes along.

The very first experiences an infant has in the church nursery will have a strong effect on how that child perceives the church from then on. If the child feels security and acceptance, he or she will transfer those feelings to all other relationships in the church. Parents (especially with their first child) are apprehensive about leaving their infants in a new environment; so a comfortable, welcoming setting will relieve their fears about separating from an infant. For some people the church nursery is the first child care they have ever tried beyond close friends or members of their extended family. So the church school offers a marvelous opportunity for young children to begin to learn to associate with a group of children their own age in a short-term, limited-size group. The Sunday school experience can therefore prepare the child to enjoy preschool and kindergarten settings.

As children begin to mature and communicate, they have a way of asking very complex questions about faith. While these seem "complex" to parents and other adults, they are quite simple and logical to the child. When a young child begins to ask, "What keeps the moon up in the sky?" or "What happened to Grandpa when he died?" adults stammer and grasp for answers that can satisfy the child's curiosity and yet not be so filled with myth that the child will have to unlearn that idea later in life.

The young child is filled with energy, very curious, growing rapidly, learning to use large and small muscles, seeking to exert his or her own autonomy—to become an individual person separate from parents and siblings. The two basic thrusts—the parents' hope for passing on an adequate faith and the child's probing curiosity—make the nursery and preschool programs of the church very important.

Effective Christian education methods as well as authentic evangelistic strategies can be designed only when they address the real developmental characteristics of young children. Let us first examine these roadsigns of development in infants and toddlers before looking at the preschooler and kindergartner.

Roadsigns for Understanding Infants and Toddlers

Emotional Development

Children from birth to age two need to develop the confidence that they are loved and that their world is trustworthy. If we help young children to develop, they will later transfer these feelings toward God. The first experiences of love and trust begin to build the foundations for faith even in the youngest infants.

Babies and toddlers have certain routines at home that help them develop a sense of trust. The caregiver in the church nursery who follows the same routine is helping the young child develop a sense that the world (created by God) is dependable and safe.

Because preschool children are also becoming individuals, independent of their parents, the social conditions of the Sunday school are very important. For the infant and the very young child the nursery of the Sunday school must be a warm and welcoming place. The rooms must be comfortable, with toys and furniture that are inviting. All attendants and teachers must be caring and thoughtful individuals who welcome each child. Each child should feel free to leave its parents for short periods so they can begin to associate with others in groups. This requires a clean and familiar environment where the infant's cries are quickly responded to.

Theological Development

Through being loved, children can learn that God is love. In the church we cannot give "faith" to children as we would any other commodity or gift, but we do provide the atmosphere in which the child can develop its own faith. Children begin to hear the word *God* and do not know what it means, but they realize that God and Jesus are special. Each time you provide a simple snack for toddlers, a simple prayer will help them understand that we thank this loving God for food.

Social Development

The teachers and nursery caregivers must understand that two-year-olds are generally too young to know how to share toys, that they usually play beside other children rather than with them. It is only when they become three- and four-year-olds that they begin to share and play together. We need not place unwarranted expectations on the behavior of these younger children. Sharing the Christian faith is first built on having a safe and encouraging environment.

Stepping Stones to Church School Attendance

In light of the developing needs of young children and their parents, we list a few ideas that should help increase the attendance of nursery and toddler children. One will not be able to encourage each child directly to make a decision about attendance. The efforts made to increase the attendance at this age level will have a slower, less direct impact on that attendance. At the same time, studies have shown that the parents of this age group are the most "ready" to begin coming to church and Sunday school and to bring their children.

1. Provide a clean and well-equipped nursery. First impressions may be the most powerful and lasting ones on any newcomer. It cannot be stated too strongly that the nursery area must appear clean and tidy. Look over your inventory of toys to see that all are safe and that there are enough pieces in order for each toy to be played with properly. Toys should not be so complicated that younger children will not be able to enjoy them.

When parents arrive at the nursery, they should be able to tell quickly what they need to do in order to leave their child. There could be a desk or table close to the door for attendants to register each child and to check in the equipment and supplies that parents have brought for the child. Then the parents will need to see where the child will be cared for and where they can pick up the child when Sunday services are over.

The name of each attendant should also be in a prominent place for the parents to see and remember. For churches that use the same attendants each week, a poster with the names can be placed on the door. If you have some rotation of child care workers the attendants should regularly wear a clear name tag.

Attendants for infants need to follow healthy practices for changing and storing or discarding soiled diapers. They must use thorough hygiene habits and be sure to wash between times they care for different children. If a nursery is apt to be used at other times during the week than just on Sunday morning, one should be sure that a janitor is prepared to check it out regularly so that it is nearly always clean and attractive.

2. Use clear signs and greeters to direct persons to the nursery. Location of the nursery is important as well. If possible, the best location for the nursery is close to the primary entrance used by those persons who come to Sunday school. The second choice is close to the church's sanctuary entrance. Many times it is helpful to indicate in the Sunday worship bulletin that nursery child care is available and to indicate how parents can locate the nursery. There should be plenty of posters or directional signs around the church to lead first-timers to the nursery. Finally, greeters are also helpful to newcomers to assist them to find the proper room.

There are a few parents of infants who may prefer to hold their child throughout a Sunday school class or worship service. Do not be surprised at this. Many parents who both work do not want to be separated from their child on Sunday morning. As the weeks go by and the newborn begins to squirm and becomes difficult to keep quiet throughout a class time, the parent is likely then to begin placing the infant in the church's care.

3. Record the names, addresses, ages, and instructions for child care indicated by the parents. The single most important factor in whether or not parents return is if they find that their child has been made to feel comfortable and that all instructions for her or his care have been graciously followed. It is also important to have facts— names, etc.—in case the visitors decide not to register in the adult class or worship service. These records can be used to send notices of upcoming events.

4. Provide quality adult classes for parents. For newcomers who are not used to the habits of Sunday morning activities of getting up early, dressing their children, and loading up to attend religious services, there needs to be a strong attraction for them at Sunday school as well as comfortable care for their children. The chapter on younger and middle adults gives some suggestions for ways to start new classes for these persons.

5. Provide guidance classes and helpful materials to assist in being effective parents. This is an important service the church can provide for parents. Some church school curriculums have resources on parenting for these persons, but leaders of the church school that wants to grow will probably have to do some of their own research on the kinds of resources that will appeal to the parents of their church school.

The most helpful kinds of resources are likely to be those that address the stages of development of infants and toddlers or advise young families on starting traditions or rituals that will introduce the Christian faith to their children.

The parents of toddlers will also appreciate knowing the kind of information that is being taught in the Sunday school. In one preschool, the director met parents as they loaded children into cars to tell them just what had occurred that day in class. This kind of information is a real gift to the parents of very young children—who are so interested in sharing the moments of joy and discovery with their child. Many children are not able to remember what they have studied or to explain exactly what they have done, so when the parents ask, "What did you do today?" the child only replies, "Nothing."

6. See that adequate child care is provided for all programs or services of the church. If one's church has not had many young adults or children in church school, the Christian education department or council will need to keep reminding other leaders in the church to provide child care during all of its other services. Include high chairs and booster seats even for toddlers who visit the adult worship services. Many leaders don't remember what it was like to have young children in their church. Other activities in the church's program will also have an impact on whether or not newcomer parents will choose to join your church school.

7. Insist on qualified, trained caregivers for the nursery. These attendants must enjoy young children and their fears, their spilled messes, their short tempers, their curiosity for exploring out-of-the-way places, and their experimenting with loud noises. These persons must be able to communicate an air of competency and a spirit of welcome to the parents as well. In order to experience growth in the nursery and toddler classes, attendants need to tell the parents how their child has acted during the time the parents were away.

The caregivers should make a special effort to speak directly to each child, no matter how young, as each leaves the nursery. Be sure to make eye contact and invite each one to come back again soon.

8. Provide resources and services to your neighborhood. A congregation should let the community know that its church school cares about all families, that it is willing to provide the services they need to cope in today's world. Following is a list of the kinds of programs that might be considered as an outreach to families around the church and throughout the community. In order for them to have an impact on church school attendance, one will need to ask whether or not the church really wants those children in the church school and what will be done to bridge the gaps between the community families and the church.

—Preschool, day care, or story hours.
—Mother's day out, father's evening out, child care for parent's Saturday shopping.
—Child care for mothers going back to school.
—Loaner car seats for transporting newborns home from the hospital.

The particular kind of outreach a church might consider must not only match the community's urgent needs, but a church school's space, equipment, financial resources, and volunteer personnel as well.

Overcoming Stumbling Blocks

Several weaknesses appear in Sunday schools that serve as barriers or stumbling blocks to visitors. The best solution to such barriers is knowing that they exist or preventing their happening in the first place.

The following stumbling blocks might need special attention because they have a great impact on children as well as their parents.

So Where Is the Nursery?

In many churches the nursery location was selected for its proximity to the other children's classrooms or to the restrooms. However, for most newcomers this means that the nursery is out of the way and difficult to find.

Solution: Locate the nursery as nearly as possible to the main entrance of the church. If this is not possible, provide lots of posters and signs indicating just where the nursery can be found. For many visitors it is also important to be able to find the most appropriate classroom for their other children and for themselves.

Remember that parents who have their hands full of children's coats, diaper bags, their own purses, and even the hand of an older child need ready assistance as quickly as possible. While signs can be most useful to the visitor, there is nothing to compare with the personal touch of a real, live greeter.

Broken Toys and "Hand-Me-Down" Equipment

Nothing signals a new parent that things are not right so much as the presence of old, broken toys, and rough, outmoded furniture and play equipment. Toys and equipment should be limited to the kind that match the age level of the children assigned to that room. A room that appears not to be clean or well kept may send shivers of fear in the hearts of young parents when leaving their child. Dirty conditions seem to be an open invitation to lots of childhood germs and viruses.

Solution: One solution to this problem is to have a parents' and teachers' clean-up day. Fresh paint will cover a lot of ugly walls. Be sure that the decorations (pictures or posters) that adorn the wall are contemporary and not outdated nursery-rhyme characters. It is better to spend a few dollars on new child-oriented posters than to have outmoded pictures. A school supply store is a good source of such decorations.

Mixing Toddlers with Crib Babies

Newcomers will also be afraid to leave a young infant if it appears that toddlers can wander up to a crib and touch or awaken a sleeping infant. There are also fears of passing colds, and some will be concerned about their child's safety.

Another stumbling block is the evidence that the room is over-crowded. This not only evokes the fear that the infant might be bothered by an older child; it also makes a parent wonder if their child will have its needs met in a quick and efficient manner.

Solution: If infants in cribs and older toddlers need to share the same room, there are a number of ways that the furniture can be arranged to restrict the movement of toddlers. Place several rocking chairs between the toddlers' play area and the cribs, or bring in short bookcases to store toys that can only be reached from the side facing away from the infant cribs.

If the room becomes too crowded one might first eliminate any play structures that encourage large energetic types of play: e.g. a children's slide or rocking horse. Most playpens are used only to collect toys and they take up a large amount of needed space.

Another solution might be to reassign age levels throughout the preschool area so that some children can be moved out of the nursery area into a room for the next age level. Some functions of the nursery can be moved out into the hall, for example, where the coats are stored or where certain supplies are kept. Sometimes closets can have their doors removed and be converted to toy storage that is accessible to children, eliminating the need for storage units. The greatest space consumer in most church nurseries are large classroom tables. Replacing them with several small tables may gain more room.

Finally, remember that the ratio of children to the adult attendants significantly affects the quality of child care. The recommended ratio is one adult for every three infants and one adult for every two toddlers.

In a few churches too many teenagers are allowed to spend their free time in the nursery and toddler rooms when they are not needed. Their presence may actually contribute to the natural confusion that is already there.

Using these stepping stones and eliminating these stumbling blocks may begin to help Sunday school grow. More important, they will increase the effectiveness of the educational ministry with infants and toddlers.

Roadsigns for Understanding
Preschool and Kindergarten Children

Let us now turn our attention to the older children that are preschool age.

Social Development

As children begin to grow into the preschool years they are learning to be social creatures with other children, with brothers and sisters, and with adults other than parents. They begin to share toys and to play together. They will develop close attachments as first friends to one or two other classmates. It is an extra bonus if these friends are in the Sunday school together. Encourage families to invite such friends to their homes for play time together.

The preschool child is learning cooperation and negotiation skills. The Sunday school needs to be a welcome place where children will be permitted to experiment with new behaviors and will experience forgiveness for failures and the encouragment to try again.

Physical Development

Preschool children need large play spaces because they are mostly developing control of their large muscles. The fine motor skills associated with writing and coloring, or even cutting paper with scissors, are not well developed until about age five. This occurs sooner for girls than for boys. When a Sunday school teacher plans only activities that require cutting or drawing, it increases the child's sense of incompetence and causes much frustration. Times for quiet play and story time should be balanced with active times for using whole body movement for expression of growing arms and legs.

Intellectual Development

It is characteristic of young children's thinking that they are not "logical" in the same sense that an older child is. For example, they cannot grasp the difference between events that occurred ten years ago and ones that happened 1,000 years ago. Similarly, they cannot distinguish between fact and myth. (They believe in Santa Claus.) The church school should be careful not to teach some symbolic concept of faith in a way that will have to be unlearned later.

Preschool and kindergarten children at this age can begin to appreciate the stories of the characters of the Bible but will get ages and stages mixed up. Similarly, they have no real grasp of the laws of physics that we so clearly understand and rely upon; therefore they easily believe the miracle stories. They are full of wonder and awe and are deeply interested in nature and its many secrets. These wonders are easily explained as having come from a Creator God who also cares for them.

It is helpful to remember that all children do not develop at the same rate and that not all children are adept with their speech, especially when speaking to persons that they might not know very well, such as the church school teacher. Teachers and attendants must not always expect the children to be able to share their ideas or to discuss important facts in the total group.

Theological Development

The greatest truth of faith that parents and the church school can teach is that each person is unique and precious in God's sight, that God intends for all children to be treated with care and dignity. This learning is best taught by Bible stories and by the style of teaching in the classroom—in a climate of acceptance and caring.

The celebrations of the church year can also be fine tools for teaching faith to preschool children. They allow opportunities to act out important truths in the family life at home as well as at the church. These holidays make wonderful times to assist young families to establish their own family traditions with religious ceremonies, etc. The Advent wreath at home is a popular example.

Stepping Stones to Church School Growth

The Sunday school for preschool and kindergarten children is more apt to grow if we select stepping stones that match children's developmental needs and abilities and if we assist parents in their desire to make the church an important ingredient in their child's life. Several of these stepping stones are the same or are quite similar to those listed for infants and toddlers earlier in this chapter. But they bear repeating in this section so that a complete approach will be kept in mind by the reader.

1. Have clean, well-equipped rooms. The same standards of cleanliness are needed in the kindergarten as in the younger children's nursery. This includes outdoor playground equipment as well. For some children their first impression of any new church is the interest generated by the outdoor play equipment they see as they approach the building. The parents will notice also whether that equipment is safe and well protected from auto traffic or if it is accessible to older children and hence somewhat unsafe for their child.

The first sight of the classroom should appeal to a child's sense of curiosity, excitement, and wonder. The preschool and kindergarten rooms need colorful children's art or other appropriate decorations. Normally it is best to use neutral colors of paint for the walls and ceilings so that they reflect the light properly. The bright colors that we associate with cheerfulness and with children are best provided in pictures and other decorations or else the rooms will seem too busy. Bulletin boards, chalkboards, and posters should be at children's eye level.

It is also important to have the right-sized equipment in the room. However, a lot of improvising can be done before a church school needs to invest in lots of new and costly furniture. One creative church made a large indoor "sandbox" with Styrofoam packing pellets rather than sand. These are easy to clean up and they do not stick to the children's clothes. The rooms should have a well-planned arrangement so that there are plenty of separate play centers with a variety of activities: puzzles, costumes, home care toys, art easels, books, etc. Variety can be achieved if these centers are changed occasionally.

2. Use a thorough system of registering the attendance. This must include a way to recognize visitors and to follow up on their visit; methods for follow-up on those who have missed lately; and a system to send cards, etc., and to celebrate birthdays. Children do not normally receive mail addressed directly to them. A postcard that comes in the mail addressed with his or her name in large print can be a very impressive gift to the young child. Even though most of these children do not yet read, they recognize their own names when they are printed.

This system can also utilize attendance charts on the walls where the children can mark their coming to Sunday school.

Remember that some young children will be more comfortable attending a class with an older sibling than with an entirely new social group of strangers. This should be perfectly acceptable for the short term while the younger child becomes familiar with the surroundings and better acquainted with how we do things in Sunday school. Later, the older brother or sister can leave when the younger one feels secure and feels like he or she belongs.

3. Use plain directional signs throughout the building. This principle is listed in several places throughout this book. For kindergarten through all elementary grades, the signs on the doorways to each classroom should be at the children's eye level. It is helpful to list ages for each class on the signs. Teachers' names should be visible to the parents.

4. Plan occasions when parents will be invited to spend some time in the Sunday school classroom. This is important because studies of growing church schools show that one of the most influential factors is the level of "satisfaction" of the parents. This might include periodic open house programs; recruiting one set of parents to visit and assist each week; a special program that the children have practiced; or some special church holiday that lends itself to a family celebration designed by your Sunday school. Other events could be a playlet with puppets done by the children or a breakfast to celebrate Thanksgiving or Mother's Day.

5. Provide resources to help parents learn to be more effective. This could include a lending library of books. It could mean providing a subscription to a valuable parent's magazine for each family. It could mean offering specially designed courses for parents. Some popular subjects might be:
    —"safe child" protection
    —initiating family rituals with religious meaning at holidays
    —discipline without spanking
    —selecting the proper preschool
    —helping a child enter first grade
    —siblings without rivalry.

6. Provide resources for children. This could include a lending library of children's books—especially books with religious content that would not normally be available to the preschool child elsewhere. These children are also fond of records or even videos of Bible stories.
    One creative idea is to provide a traveling suitcase of special games, books, and puzzles to loan to a sick child or to one who expects to be confined for some days.

7. Publicize all church events to parents, announcing precisely what child care is (or is not) to be provided. Send any visitors or recent newcomers to the church school a letter or make a phone call to describe what normally occurs at such events, what kind of clothes people usually wear (dress or casual) and exactly how long the programs (especially evening programs) are likely to last.

8. In larger churches it is particularly helpful to use name tags on the children. This assists the teacher to call each child's given name and to help each one feel more acceptance and comfort. Use large letters so they can be read from across the room.

9. Plan occasional extended experiences for kindergarten children. In this setting they can become better acquainted with others their own age, and they can be more comfortable with their adult teachers. Examples might include Halloween and Valentine Day parties.

10. Provide guidance to visitors and relatively new parents on the church's (denomination's) practices of the sacraments and other religious celebrations. Remember that Christian education is not only nurture; it is also discipling—helping children and adults to become fully a part of the community of faith.

Overcoming Stumbling Blocks

Late, Indifferent, and Unprepared Teachers

The teacher needs to be in his or her room at least fifteen minutes before the first child arrives so that the lights are on, the temperature is set, and the room is arranged for this day's lesson. Supplies and equipment should already be in place so that when the child arrives, the teacher can greet the child and not be distracted. Good teachers will even have a special activity or surprise for that first child who arrives early. A dark or locked Sunday school room will be scary to a child and discouraging to parents.

A child will learn some lesson, no matter how ill- or well-prepared the teacher. If the teacher is ready for the children to arrive, children will learn to trust the church, will have their fears relieved, and will have a good chance of remembering the lesson. If the teacher is not prepared, the child will learn that the church is "not very important," that people who attend are not very important, and that people who greet you do not much care whether you are around at all. They may even ask, "Does God care if I am around?"

Solution: Help the teachers to see the value in their work. Train them in writing guidelines and planning activities that will add zest to the teaching. Add someone as an assistant in the class.

Classes with Too Many Children

A few Sunday schools will have had such an influx of new children in their kindergarten rooms that there are soon too many to handle well in a group.

Solution: Increase the number of attendants, find places in the hallways for some activities, make frequent "field trips" outdoors or to other places around the church, and do not have all the children on the same activity at the same time (such as hand craft). Use more stories and music activities, and less art work done at tables. Reduce the number of tables and easels, move any portable cupboards out into the hallways, and hang coats in the hallways. Divide the age levels differently; for example, during the fall the older kindergarten children and early first-graders are similar enough to be grouped together.

Conclusion

Attendance of the children in the nursery, preschool, and kindergarten in the church school will depend upon the quality of child care and whether each child feels welcomed and cherished. The persons who will be judging whether or not the child has such a quality experience will be the parents.We must be profoundly sensitive to the parents as well as to the children. If parents find excitement, joy, and support, and their child seems to enjoy Sunday school, they are likely to return and join.

The other, equally important ingredient that influences attendance of children is whether or not the adults who bring them also have a positive experience of their own in church school. The work of the preschool department goes hand-in-hand with the work of the adult departments.

According to the population statistics and the religious attitude surveys, we should expect this age level to be one of the fastest growing segments of the churches over the next decade. Let us be conscientious to make sure that we are prepared to "welcome one such child" in Christ's name (Matthew 18:5).

6

Elementary Children

Jesus said, "Let the children come to me and do not stop them, because the Kingdom of heaven belongs to such as these."
—Matthew 19:14, TEV

The way we promote church school attendance teaches who we are as the church.
—Linda Chenoweth

As the church school looks to its future and asks whether it is possible to get young children into its classes, it is very heartening to know that there are two great trends in today's world that promise to produce greater involvement for these children: (a) The total number of children in the lower elementary grades is rapidly growing because of the increased birth rate in recent years. (b) The parents of these children, most of whom are among the youngest of the "baby boomers" born after World War II, are committed to provide religious and moral education for their children. The evidence suggests that, if your church school prepares itself for growth, plans better methods to convince visitors to return, and discovers new ways to invite new children to Sunday school, your church can experience new vitality and increased attendance.

Road Signs for Understanding
Elementary Children

When children begin the first grade and master the art of reading, their rate of learning seems to explode. Growing children make a great number of changes as they move from the first through the sixth grades. The church school must adapt its teaching style to each of these changes in order to be able to serve effectively the growing spiritual needs of the elementary child.

Physical Development

One word best describes the elementary school age children—*active!* They are mastering both large muscle skills and fine motor skills. These children begin to do well at baseball and soccer and at the same time are better able to draw, write, play an instrument, or operate a computer keyboard. They enjoy the challenge of learning.

Social Development

Elementary children seek the approval and avoid the disapproval of significant adults. The teacher must be cautious never to use sarcasm and put-downs to control behavior. Positive regard is the best motivator of learning.

As they grow, they become more aware of the distinction between the sexes, and by the sixth grade some have even begun to enter puberty.

Elementary children begin to develop order and organization in their lives. They take control of their own schedules. They want to be treated "fairly," a word they frequently use to describe how they want to be dealt with. This fairness also comes into play in their growing sense of rivalry and competition between themselves and others, whether in sports or in the search for approval of peers and adults. They insist on playing by the rules and they want all rules to be applied equally to all children.

Intellectual Development

For the first time the elementary child begins to understand the concept of history and the eras of the world. This is the best time to teach about the difference between the Old and the New Testaments, even to develop a time line for the chronology of the Bible.

They have a great curiosity and become natural collectors: stamps, baseball cards, souvenirs, etc. Classification of events, ideas, and Bible personalities is very interesting to this age. The imagination is much more controlled, as evidenced by their overcoming their fear of the dark and its imagined monsters. Because elementary children who are pre-puberty are in the quiet stages of maturation called "latency" they are not so consumed by the changes in their bodies as is true of other ages such as two-years-olds or adolescents. For this reason there is more chance for them to memorize factual information.

Spiritual Development

As they develop, elementary children can begin to appreciate the great events of the Bible. They easily memorize facts. They begin to understand the importance of symbols. This kind of abstract thinking is the necessary transition stage for them to be able to come to their own personal convictions about faith. Care must be taken to encourage individual thinking.

Elementary children must also be helped to learn to express their thoughts; they are not good at speeches or writing down what they believe. They need other means of self-expression such as service projects, art, music, drama, poetry, making gifts, etc.

Educational Directions for Elementary Children

Build upon the skills already learned. Elementary children are just developing their skill of reading and are gaining greater physical control over their large and small muscle actions. Educational methods that take advantage of these growing skills will not only rely upon their ears for listening to the lesson. They will take advantage of the child's whole body as a resource by which to learn. They will use the eyes to read, to see visuals and videotapes. They will use their hands for drawing, sculpting, writing or computing, for this builds on their own skills. By contrast, elementary children do not have well developed skills for discussion. That skill develops as they begin to mature into adolescence.

Teach the Ten Commandments and the golden rule. Because children this age find it reassuring to shape their behavior with rules, the rules of the Bible can be effectively taught to them. At the same time they are also more aware of their social relationships. They can understand norms of human interaction. Therefore, elementary children can begin to appreciate and learn the importance of the standards for living taught by the Bible, especially by Jesus. They can also begin to recognize what forgiveness truly means. Stories and parables from the Bible are their most effective teachers. They can understand and appreciate biblical rules and can order their lives through clear guidelines.

Teach with adventure stories of the Bible. The children have wonderful imaginations and yet they also think in very concrete terms. They enjoy learning through the adventures of the heroes of the Bible. Because they can easily place themselves in the role of other characters, they love drama and the pageantry of the Bible. Puppets, drama, posters, games, and artwork are all effective teachers.

Develop the children's ability to learn through symbols. Because the youngest elementary children are not ready to think in abstract terms, much of the symbolism of the church is confusing to them. They are capable, however, of memorizing some signs so that they can remember particular meanings given to specific symbols that the church uses. A first-grader, for example, can remember that grapes are used to make the wine of communion. Sixth-graders, on the other hand, will comprehend the ways that the wine of communion represents Christ's sacrifice.

Still, as the children begin to mature we must help them begin to learn how symbols teach us new ideas. This will help them be prepared to understand the more abstract concepts that the Christian faith relies upon. The order of the holidays of the Christian year provide a wonderful framework to begin teaching such symbolism.

Stepping Stones to Church School Attendance

Any growth in the church school will begin slowly and will develop best as new members who join the Sunday school begin to have wonderful experiences and are encouraged to invite their friends to join them. Remember also that we have to have a fine program in place before we invite them or we will not have earned the right to expect them to return. Some congregations have tried a new approach for inviting children from their neighborhoods by advertising their summer vacation church schools, only to be shocked to find their publicity was such a success that too many new children showed up. They did not have enough adult leadership to guarantee a good experience. As a result, the children never came back to Sunday school.

Here are a few ideas.

1. Develop a list of prospects. Many Sunday schools are convinced that there are really few prospects for their Sunday school. This is especially true if few young families or young children have visited the Sunday school over the past several years. Here are a few possibilities for getting names of children to invite.

—Ask members for names of their grandchildren.
—Ask members in the young adult and middle adult classes for friends within their own network who have children not now attending Sunday school. Maybe they know someone who recently moved to town or was divorced.
—Provide after-school programs for children in the community. Concentrate on the skills of volunteers in the church. Some examples might be art clubs, Boy Scouts, Girl Scouts, music and drama clubs, or tutoring programs.
—Ask school teachers, social workers, and counselors in the community or the church if they know children who would enjoy and benefit from joining your church school activities.
—Make up a new subcommittee whose only job is to find the names of prospects, to see that they are invited and to provide the needed transportation.

2. Set attendance goals, using charts to demonstrate progress. This is the easiest way to see the consistency with which each child attends. It can also alert the teacher to follow up on the child who has been absent. Such charts, as well, demonstrate to each student that regular attendance is important. By setting goals for increasing attendance the teacher can also teach the children to invite their friends to join them in church.

3. Give the students continuing projects that require them to attend several sessions in a row. Developing consistent attendance is an important ingredient in the effectiveness of the learning process. It also is one of the first ways to increase the total attendance figures of your Sunday school.

4. Keep accurate records on each child, with parents' names, addresses, telephone numbers, names of brothers and sisters, and birthdates. This kind of information is invaluable to teachers as they begin a new season with new classes. It also sets the framework for the teacher to be able to establish personal rapport with each child. A caring and supporting relationship between teacher and pupil encourages regular attendance and is extremely important to good learning.

5. Plan for activities with the children outside the regular Sunday morning class time. This allows for more informal learning to occur and for developing that caring relationship between the teacher and the student. Programs might be field trips, a children's choir, hobby clubs, seasonal parties, or service projects for the church or neighborhood.

6. Involve the children in planning what and how they will be learning. This is an important skill for any teacher who hopes to get full involvement of the students with the subject. It also invites students to be more commited and involved in class. If the children have a positive experience, they will be better able to tell others about their Sunday school and will be more inclined to bring their friends along.

7. Follow up immediately on all visitors. This means that during the class session the teacher must take care to learn the visitors' names and some way to include them in the lesson. Sometimes the teacher may want to spend a few moments at the end of the class session becoming better acquainted and to let the child know how much he or she is welcome in the class. It is important to make some contact later to let visitors know, again, that you are truly pleased that they chose to attend your class.

If the child visited as the result of an invitation from another class member, it is important to express appreciation to that child as well.

8. Keep in regular contact with parents. Research suggests that parents' satisfaction with a Sunday school has a great deal of influence on whether or not they invite other families to attend. It also affects their sense of the importance of seeing that their children are consistent in attendance.

Regular communication with the parents will let them know what the class is doing and what their child is learning. It is also an excellent opportunity to advise some parents on matters relating to their job of parenting. Sometimes the Sunday school is the one place where children are able to be fully accepted and to excel if, in their other schooling, they are graded much below their peers and hence suffer from low self-esteem. Contact with parents raises the teacher's awareness of any particular need of a child that might call for the teacher to make special arrangements.

Of course, the best contacts with parents are personal conversations after the class meets or at other church meetings. Other opportunities to talk could be at some event such as Little League baseball games or school activities. The teacher might make a special appointment to visit in the child's home.

Other contacts could be made through notes sent home with the child or mailed to the parents. These notes could contain reprints from magazine articles or teacher manuals that contain helpful ideas for parenting.

Some Sunday schools have found that hosting an open house in the classroom once or twice a year is a great benefit. Another contact could be initiated by asking the parent to take a turn assisting in the classroom or in planning a social event outside the classroom hour.

9. Display the children's artwork throughout the church. Not only does this encourage the children to feel good about their Sunday school work, it lets the rest of the congregation know that there is growth and progress in the children's departments of the church.

10. Provide transportation when necessary. For some churches in the last decade this meant that every growing church school must have fleets of buses for bringing children to church. Today, this approach seems like "overkill." Yet the principle of helping children be consistent in attendance is an important approach to increasing church school attendance.

In some families, when a child is shared from weekend to weekend between divorced parents, another church member may be willing to pick up this child in order for him or her to attend on the weekend spent with the parent who is not interested in the church school. For other families, it is difficult to arrange transportation for one child when another is ill. Assistance in getting the well child to church can be a wonderful relief for the parent tied down with sick children at home.

This reponsibility should not fall entirely upon the teachers. It is a task that could well be shared by the parents of other pupils. There also may be some older adult, who would enjoy this kind of responsibility.

11. Be sure that the classrooms are clean and well-equipped with modern teaching furniture and resources. Public education for children in these times is very sophisticated. The church must keep pace or children will be bored and feel out of place. The most important ingredient for children is to feel that they are important.

12. See that child care and programs for children are included during all adult functions at your church. Parents who visit a church will begin to drop away if there are not provisions made for their children when there are programs that are of primary interest to adults. If parents have to hire babysitters and provide child care at home every time there is a function they want to attend, they will become discouraged and begin looking for another church where their children are included.

13. Involve children in the total worship life of the congregation. Over the next few years this may be the most significant factor that will separate those churches that are growing from those that are merely stable or even declining. Not only do children learn the faith from viewing adults at worship, involving children shows that the congregation cherishes their presence.

14. Use special events as an extra inducement to encourage Sunday school children to invite their friends to visit. Such events could be Halloween parties, summer camps, and vacation church schools. They might be a Scout Sunday or any other kinds of programs. People seem to feel more comfortable inviting friends to attend a less "religious" event than a regular worship service. Parties and social affairs allow more time for getting acquainted, time for a sense of belonging to develop gradually.

15. Plan for some delight or surprise for the children in each class session. Part of the gift of childhood is the chance to experience the awe of first experiences, the mystery and celebration of new discoveries. This can greatly enhance the readiness of each child to participate in the learning. If the classroom teacher can capitalize on the elementary child's excitement in new experiences, she or he will be able to increase the readiness for the adventure of learning.

Overcoming Stumbling Blocks

Drab Surroundings

Every experienced teacher can testify to the fact that pleasant surroundings greatly enhance the learning climate in a classroom. They also increase the likelihood that children will enjoy their experience and will be more apt to keep their attendance regular. It is very easy for adults to see only the larger picture and to accept the fact that there may not be enough funds to have a new paint job or to secure the nicest new furniture. The conscientious teacher may overlook the inconvenience of a drab or dark classroom and soon learn to ignore its depressing effect. Yet we constantly have to view the classroom setting through the eyes of the children, especially through those of a newcomer, in order to overcome a poor environment that hampers learning and discourages excitement.

Solution: One way to make an immediate change in the character of a drab classroom is to throw away or store any equipment and furniture that is not absolutely necessary. This will give a new openness to the room. Each class may utilize some furniture during certain time periods while other furniture is stored and then change it for other times of the year.

For some rooms a new coat of paint may be the quickest and easiest solution. Adding a new coat of paint to a room may be a great way to involve some of the children's parents, as well. Alert the teachers to have a greater sensitivity to the setting and its affect on their attitudes and on the pleasure of the students.

Lack of Teachers

This is a recurrent problem for the board or department of Christian education. Yet, there seems to be a correlation between the willingness of persons to accept a call to be a teacher and the quality of the teaching that currently prevails in that Sunday school. Sunday schools that seem to raise a great sense of excitement in the pupils, where parents are pleased with their children's experience, have an easier time recruiting teachers than do those where people feel it is a pretty sad program.

Solution: Make sure that every person who is recruited to serve as a teacher is convinced that teaching is a very important task and that the Sunday school expects each volunteer to give the very best. Quality seems to beget quality; images of positive strengths in a congregation seem to generate more feelings that there is value in the work of teaching. The best place to introduce new persons to teaching is to recruit them to serve in the summer Sunday school program, which has a limited time commitment, or during vacation church school. In both of these situations there is more time to observe each new person's skills in order to select the best type of leader. These occasions also provide more opportunity than the programs during the school year for training in skills needed for creative teaching.

Neglect by Teachers

In some church schools the teachers have been serving in the same position for so long that they have lost their interest and enthusiasm for new ideas that will encourage greater attendance. This discouragement can be easily sensed by the students—either consciously or unconsciously.

It is the responsibility of the board or department of Christian education to be alert to such teachers and to find ways to ease their load and to compensate for their despair with programs or events for the children beyond the regular class time.

Solution: For some teachers, a new assistant will serve as a breath of fresh air and will rejuvenate their energy. For others, the apathy will probably degenerate until they ask to be relieved from their task. Then they can be replaced by new persons who can be trained to generate enthusiasm. For still others, the best tactic is to ask them to begin to assume more leaderhip in training new teachers or to participate in the larger plans for the entire program of Christian education.

Sometimes burnout can be prevented by making clear to new teachers before they take their job that the church school expects them to fulfill their responsibility for increasing attendance as well as just teaching a lesson from the curriculum materials. For many classes the work of planning for increasing attendance can best be done by an assistant that works regularly with the lead teacher. Teachers become willing workers if they feel that the entire congregation strongly supports all their efforts.

For teachers to fulfill their assignments about boosting attendance, they must have a ready supply of all the needed materials. If the church school expects each teacher to keep accurate rolls, then full class lists with names and addresses should be provided for the teacher before meeting the class for the first time. If the teacher is expected to send postcards to children who miss, then the church school must be sure that those cards with the appropriate postage are always kept in adequate supply.

Too Small a Class

In some cases, when the church has a tradition about how many different age-level classes must be offered, a church school will end up with one or two very small classes. This can be discouraging for the teachers. They may even spend several Sundays wondering if they really need to prepare a lesson because there might not be many children. The children then become very self-conscious about participating in such a class, especially if they fear their teacher is likely to ask a lot of questions in order to get them to discuss.

When either the teacher or the students fear small groups there is discouragement and this blocks increased attendance. Why would a student in this kind of a class want to invite a visitor?

Solution: The new curriculums offer advice for joining several age levels into a broadly graded class. Each year you might change the age distribution for a better balance in the size of room you have.

Even though there are few students, it still behooves a teacher to try to utilize many different teaching styles and methods so that the students are convinced that they are doing important and even "fun" learning activities. This will take some creativity. Having fewer students will allow a teacher to take the class on field trips, or to meet in rooms of the church that a larger group could not manage.

There are some teachers who may actually prefer smaller classes. Those who do so often tell how much more flexible and creative they can be with only a few students. Those churches with small memberships can give great testimony to the power that comes from such small groups.

Wrong-Size Furniture

Nothing speaks of neglect for the student quite like worn out or wrong-size furniture.

Solution: Use learning activities that do not require a lot of time spent sitting at such furniture or writing and drawing on uneven tabletops. Start using a rug so that the children can spend some time sitting on the floor or ask the children to bring cushions from home. Have more movement so the whole time is not spent at one place in the room. Throw away old furniture; ask for contributions from members of the church. Even move the class to other places in the church for occasional variety. Be sure that visitors will be able to find the new location.

Lack of Variety in Teaching Methods

This problem is very similar to others described above. It would appear that the primary reason for this is one or more of the following:
—Teachers feel they are alsolutely bound to the lesson activities suggested by the printed curriculum. They may feel too insecure to bring in their own ideas for a new learning method.
—Teachers may have had so many discipline problems with their children that they are afraid to try anything out of the ordinary, lest their class get too rowdy and out of hand.
—The teachers do not take enough time to plan ahead to utilize a wide variety of learning activities. They begin to take short-cuts in their planning and use only the simplest of methods that do not require them to plan ahead.

Solution: Assist the teachers in long-term planning so that there can be more opportunity for variety. Recruit helpers who have special skills or projects that they can introduce to the class, such as grandpas to help with a carpentry project, someone else to teach a special musical lesson, or the minister to take the children on a tour of the church.

Lack of Parental Support

Teachers and leaders in the Sunday school will be frustrated if parents do not encourage their children in regular attendance. Parent satisfaction and parent participation with the Christian education program are absolutely crucial to the growth of a church.

Solution: Send work home with the students. This includes the projects the student has completed in class. It may also mean the kind of work that needs parental help in order to be completed before the next session.

Ask parents to help in the class occasionally. Have parents come to the class and tell how their families have established religious traditions in the home: e.g., for Advent, Easter, family birthdays, etc.

Conflicts and Interruptions in Schedule

More and more in today's society, demands on the time and interest of children increase. Even young children are encouraged to join soccer leagues that are scheduled to meet on Sunday mornings. As our society continues to grow more diverse, such conflicts will continue to grow.

Solution: Have the Christian education department do better planning, using some creativity in selecting schedules. For example, have the classes meet much earlier in the morning.

Do a better job of communicating your plans to the rest of the congregation. In some cases the department of Christian education simply does not plan early enough for a family to be able to make a wise decision in favor of the church. For example, if the Sunday school does not notify parents about the dates for vacation church school or camps by late January or February, they are likely to have already signed up their children for summer school, baseball leagues, or scout camps. If they have already placed a large financial deposit in such programs, they are not very likely to make a change later when they hear the church's dates. If they had had a choice earlier, they might have selected the church school experience.

Conclusion

The number of children who are now of elementary school age is rapidly growing. Research tells us that parents of these children have a strong desire to pass on traditional values to their children. For this reason there is likely to be an increase in the number of visitors to our Sunday schools. If we are prepared to greet and to keep these children, we can expect to see growth in our Sunday schools.

Remember, however, that growth in attendance is not the same as growth in discipleship. There are lots or proven methods simply to get children to attend. As responsible planners for the ministry of Christian education, we must plan to utilize only those methods for increasing attendance that are consistent with our church's heritage and our understanding of faith commitment.

7

Youth

"Let no one despise your youth . . . ."

—1 Timothy 4:12

The primary task of the church is the making of disciples. Accordingly, we need to accept youth as the individual people they are, help them to explore and affirm their faith, grow in their relationship with God, and become more just and loving in their relationships with their peers, their families and the world community.

—Affirmations for Youth Ministry
Thompson Center, St. Louis, Missouri

Increasing the attendance of youth in the junior high and senior high Sunday school classes of the church is a complicated and many-splendored thing. Many people are doing creative work with youth in Sunday school classes on Sunday mornings.

For some others, the Sunday school hour is the most neglected, the most dreaded, and the most boring of all times. Most of us are somewhere between these two poles.

From the image portrayed in the media, many church leaders conclude that most teenagers are self-centered and have little interest in issues of faith or religious values. However, recent research studies have shown just the opposite. Studies by such groups as the Gallup

Organization, Youth Specialities of Denver Colorado, Group Magazine, the Connecticut Mutual Life Report on American Values in the 1980s, all report that nearly half of the youth interviewed have said that they would respond if they were requested to help in the Sunday school, other church education programs, youth activities, and a variety of tasks in social service, church music, or fellowship events.

It has also been reported that the main thing youth are seeking from the church is not recreation or other activities, but spiritual nourishment. For the same reasons, adolescents are inclined to lose faith in the church because they conclude that most of the adults they are watching do not appear to take theology and spirituality very seriously.

While we will examine many issues or factors that affect the attendance of young people, there are two major influences that seem to supercede all others: (1) whether or not parents encourage their children to attend church school, even if it means rearranging family schedules; and (2) whether or not the youth were involved in any significant church programs when they were younger. When asked what he thought was the most important factor in getting youth to attend Sunday school, one friend replied "Get their parents involved."That rings very true!

The best way to develop any youth program with activities beyond the Sunday school hour is to begin with children as they are younger and bring them up into the youth program. Starting programs for children to develop friendships outside of the church school time at the younger ages will increase their loyalty when they becomeyouth.

The suggestions to increase the Sunday school attendance of youth may be helpful in one community and not in another. Size of the congregation, size of the community, number of different schools the youth attend, potential youth whose families are members of the church, whether or not the congregation has a professional staff person who is specifically assigned youth work—all these factors havean effect.

We need to be careful not to discard an idea because it appears useful only to a large congregation with its own youth minister or conversely, it sounds like it would work only in a small community. By changing or adapting the suggestions, you might come up with an effective new strategy, with some stepping stones that just fit your own Sunday school situation.

Roadsigns for Understanding Youth

There are numerous books and other resources available for those adults who work with youth in the church. Most are helpful for understanding the dynamics and forces of adolescence, the process of development of young men and women. We cannot begin to duplicate the expertise of those resources. However, the person who wants new insights on how to increase church school attendance must translate the "needs" of youth (their persistent life concerns) into specific plans that will meet those needs. What we include in this chapter are certain assumptions about youth and their needs that are of particular significance for youth in the church school.

Physical Growth

We are all familiar with the rapid growth that most youth experience. They become self-conscious about their bodies and think that everyone must be watching them. They become preoccupied with clothes and other concerns that their peers lay upon them—music, movies, grades, athletics, makeup, and dating.

Many adults have the impression that puberty or adolescence is some kind of disease. They believe that the period of maturing from childhood to adulthood is so strange that it must be a mental illness. It is as if we imagine that teenagers somehow leave the human race for six to eight years and—if all goes well—return to us later as adults.

Teenagers! Please note! Growing through adolescence is no more unusual than learning to walk, or being a "terrible two-year-old," or learning how to be married to someone, or discovering at age forty that life seems to have passed by, or being afraid and lonely when the youngest child has moved away from home for the last time, or feeling useless because of retirement. Adolescence is a healthy, hopeful transition in life that God has provided for all of us so that we may become mature, healthy, self-confident adults.

Personal Responsibility

The teenage years are often the first ones in which parents allow their child to choose whether or not he or she wants to attend church. At that time some do choose not to attend, often motivated by the simple need to make their own decisions. However, it has been demonstrated that many parents underestimate their own power to influence their children about the church. When parents fail to tell their own children how important faith and church membership are to them, they miss a great opportunity to communicate their own values at the youth's most impressionable age.

Communication with Adults

Sometimes we adults treat young people as if they are from another country and we are not able to understand or speak their language. We think that only a few parents and special teachers have the gift to talk with youth and the rest of us are inadequate. In fact, many adults are so shy around young people that they feel they do not even know how to start a conversation. This fearfulness makes the job of recruiting Sunday school teachers for youth especially difficult.

Young people sense this barrier or gap and sometimes are tempted to conclude that indeed they are unusual. They have heard this so many times they begin to believe that no adults—especially parents—are able to understand them or their problems.

Self-Esteem

Someone once said that teenagers focus their entire lives around only two questions: Who am I? and Do you like me? The first question is both a personal and a religious question and should be addressed in Sunday school. The second is a social question that needs serious attention by those workers who seek to serve youth in the church. The teenage years are a time of sifting through all that everyone else is wanting *me* to be from the *me* I want to be. The purpose of this sifting is to decide what I want *me* to be and to begin becoming that person. What can the Sunday school do?

Educational Directions for Youth

Youth need a group where they are loved. This means a church that knows each one by name and adults who listen intently when youth talk. A church must appreciate their present skills and the persons they are now! The church must provide lots of opportunities for youth to be with other teenagers. Adults must stand by and not criticize when youth are trying out new methods of human interaction.

Youth need adult Christians they can know and emulate. One significant task of adolescent development is for each individual to learn how to make significant friendships with adults other than her or his parents. The Sunday school is one of the best institutions in our society to provide opportunities for such intergenerational contact. The presence of mature and well-qualified adults is very important to an effective Sunday school for youth.

Youth need encouragement to ask questions, to think, and to search out the meaning of life. Each youth has lots of questions and needs practice at asking and seeking answers. This means asking some strange questions at times. Adults who lead youth, therefore, must be confident in their own beliefs. Because this time of questioning in life can be risky and a little bit frightening, the adults who teach teenagers need, most of all, to be supportive while also being firm about their own convictions.

Youth need a chance to be the church today. They have skills and abilities. Hence, they are confused when they are told they are the church of tomorrow as though they cannot make any significant contribution today. We are often surprised at how they truly can serve the church with their present skills. One youth class even took over the responsibility for the whole church's financial campaign when most of the adults were too burned-out or fearful about talking about money.

Youth need exposure to the richness and diversity of the whole church. This is the best age to lead persons to become familiar with the history of the church and with their own denomination by meeting significant church leaders through participation in statewide, regional, national, or even international church gatherings. Adolescence is the age of great idealism and of growing out of an ethnocentric view of life into a more universal view of the world, where different persons have different values and political philosophies. Chances to meet such people in the context of the Sunday school provide learning opportunities that are not available to most youth in today's society.

Youth need to see themselves as Christians. This may be the most important developmental task of adolescence. As young people create their own *me*, the church needs to challenge them to make definite decisions about what part Christian faith and service to the church and the world will play in their own lives. The Gallup Organization, in its 1980 survey, "The Search for America's Faith," showed that 46 percent of teenage boys and 57 percent of teenage girls would respond positively if invited to participate in a spiritual life retreat. In a similar study by C-4 Resources, 57 percent of the inactive youth in one church said they would like to help with service projects that focused on the elderly and the physically handicapped. Also, 57 percent said they would like to participate in a small Bible study group. When asked why they were no longer active in their congregation, 62 percent said church groups were too much like school and community organizations and that parties and games held little appeal for them.[1]

The church school is uniquely equipped to address these spiritual appetites that are so prevalent in today's youth.

Stepping Stones to a Growing Church School

The best methods for teaching youth in Sunday school are also the best methods to encourage youth to attend Sunday school. However, most teachers, even though they may be very creative in their teaching styles, usually neglect youth attendance issues. Some suggestions listed below are effective educational methods for the youth in the church; others are specific stepping stones to increasing attendance.

1. Have youth witness to other youth. We have long realized that young teenagers are heavily influenced in their attitudes and behaviors by their peer group, their friends. This influence is also important in recruiting youth to attend Sunday school. The best persons to invite new visitors to Sunday school will be the youth themselves.

To help youth be effective in their reaching out to others, we must not only provide a program that is appealing and challenging to those who already attend; we must also encourage them to invite their friends. Most youth are rather shy and have no idea how to go about doing this inviting. We will have to train our youth to communicate their enthusiasm for Sunday school to others.

Practice in expressing what is good about church is a good

beginning. It is also helpful for teenagers to practice talking about what faith means to themselves.

2. *Meet spiritual needs.* Some teachers and leaders think that youth today are rather self-centered and reject dealing with real faith issues. They assume that the only way to get youth interested in the church is to talk about rock and roll music, football, basketball, clothes, school activities, or MTV.

Research demonstrates that this is not the case. As mentioned on page 98, adolescents have a deep interest in religious faith, the Bible and prayer. They want religious foundations to deal with real issues of self-esteem, sexuality, justice, drugs, and alcohol abuse. They are willing to struggle to develop those foundations and to explore the implications for those tough issues in their lives.

In the same way, they do not simply care about their own needs, but they want to make a contribution to this world. In one survey of youth in the church conducted by *Group Magazine,* 47 percent of the churched teenagers said that they wish their youth groups would do more service projects; 80 percent said that the church should provide opportunities to help others; and 85 percent believe that "God wants them to spend time helping other people."[2]

The church school that tries simply to entertain its youth with parties or ski trips or that takes its lessons from popular teen magazines may develop a growing program, but it will not be an effective program for meeting the spiritual needs of adolescents.

3. *Show love and concern.* Keep attendance records. In order to help youth feel they are needed, each teacher needs to watch the attendance patterns of each person closely. By being obvious about this record keeping, the teacher demonstrates his or her conviction that regular, dependable attendance is important.

These records should also alert the teacher to the times that a particular student is apt to be absent. There are many reasons that some student could be expected to miss: One may be spending the weekend with a non-resident parent; another may have a job that occasionally forces him or her to miss; maybe the athlete has had a big game or match the day before or has one that coming afternoon; maybe the family has a lake cabin where they often spend their weekends. Well-kept attendance records can also alert a teacher that a particular student has started to drop away from church school.

Teachers who show love and concern for their students usually see better attendance. They also see their students showing a greater interest in learning. Teachers can express this love and concern by being sure to talk with each student some time each week. They can get conversations going with such questions as, "How are things going for you?" (Not just "How are you?") "How has your week gone?" "Did you get that job you were hoping for?" Try to draw each person out; ask about hobbies, if he or she got papers done, or if each enjoyed a particular outing at school.

4. Involve the parents. Not only does the Sunday school have to gain the allegiance of youth, but it also has to convince their parents that such learning is important. Sunday school will grow when parents are convinced that regular attendance is as important to their child as participation in some sport, social club, or vocational organization.

One church school has its teachers make a direct contact for an extended conversation with each set of parents to share their hopes for the class and to explain that parents must encourage the pupil to participate regularly. This kind of interview also allows time to hear from the parents their hopes and dreams for their children.

Any youth program is more apt to thrive if parents bear some of the responsibilities for the program itself: chaperoning, giving financial support, providing snacks and transportation, etc.

5. Meet needs of growing bodies. It is a well known fact that youth eat lots of food. Sometimes they are not aware of how much they do eat. The physical development of adolescents requires an incredible amount of fuel for the body. Like all other ages, youth feel more comfortable with other persons when there is a common activity to share. For most of us this is the act of sharing food together. Good refreshments can provide incentives for more regular attendance.

Adult workers can also testify to the way an otherwise cool classroom will become unbearably hot just by filling it up with adolescent bodies that are busy consuming energy for growth. Youth need a room with lots of space, comfortable furniture, and good ventilation.

6. Make goals and rules clear. Despite the way young people protest about too many rules, they are much more at home when the expectations and ground rules are clear and dependable. Youth are better able to mature when their leaders set high goals for achievement. This is just as true of Sunday school and the church as it is for sports, academics, or any other arena of effort.

If a Sunday school teacher is apologetic about the lesson or allows students to talk too long and interrupt the lesson, the young people will naturally assume it it not important to the teacher and therefore need not be important to them.

7. Use a flexible curriculum that evolves with the students' maturity. Some church school teachers try to get their teenage students to help select the weekly topics in order to generate more interest in the subjects. This is usually a wise approach. Yet, if the teacher does not inject her or his own leadership and sense of values about what youth need to learn, the pupils are apt to wash around in a pool of ignorance or to jump from one topic to another with little interest and no commitment.

Effective Sunday school teachers will constantly seek to make each lesson relevant to the everyday lives of the students, but they will also express some of their own faith and opinion. For some churches this means following the printed denominational curriculum. Others would do better by writing their own.

8. Encourage and accept lots of talking. An important task of adolescents is to adopt for themselves the values passed on from earlier generations. This means that young people need a lot of time to practice talking out what they believe, what they fear, and what they hope. They need a Sunday school where they can experiment with new words or new meanings for familiar concepts in order to express what faith means to them. Such talking is the process of learning how to incorporate new theological concepts into their own language. Only this way can those ideas become internalized.

In order to teach faith there must be time spent in learning to talk to each other in the language familiar to each person. Into this common language can be injected new concepts and new symbols (words) that represent greater spiritual meaning. For this purpose, discussion can be a most effective teaching method. Variations on this method that have appeal to different youth are singing, writing poetry, doing drama, or drawing. This requires trust among youth, trust that comes only through spending enough time together. That may mean the class needs fun and fellowship together at times other than the traditional Sunday morning hour.

9. Involve youth in the planning. One of the most important ingredients in effective teaching at all age levels is the teacher's ability to involve the students in making plans for their own learning. Give some teenagers reponsibility for the lessons and for planning what their topics will be, even having them prepare outside of class. This not only increases the receptivity for learning, it also increases their sense of satisfaction.

10. Make your program visible to the whole church. It is an old axiom that, if parents want their children to be a part of the church, they should go with them to Sunday school, not just send them. By the same token, teenagers are likely to conclude that Christian faith is not important if the whole church does not support and value the Sunday school.

Leaders of the church need to find ways to help the church show that it values the Sunday school in order to demonstrate its importance to the youth. These ten stepping stones for church school growth should assist any church school to grow in size as well as in effectiveness in creating true disciples.

Overcoming Stumbling Blocks

While it is usually most effective to initiate new steps for increasing attendance, it is also important to reduce the number of stumbling blocks that get in the way of regular attendance among youth in the church. If we do not recognize their power, we will continue to let them interfere with healthy and effective Christian education, and they will block any potential for growth in attendance. Here are a few particular blocks that are common in the youth church school classes.

Cliques

This is a common condition in most teenage groups—all groups in the church, for that matter. When one group of persons has spent a great deal of time together and enjoy each other's company, it is hard for a new person to join the group. Sometimes the presence of cliquishness within a youth group is the proof that they have experienced real Christian fellowship. However, if that experience begins to make the teenagers avoid contact with new persons, it has become a stumbling block for increasing church school attendance as well as a stumbling block for full Christian living.

Solution: This problem is one that can best be dealt with by discussing cliquish behavior as part of the Sunday school lesson. Sometimes discussion, role playing, or case studies raise the students' consciousness to the dangers of leaving someone out of discussions or activities. Values clarification exercises can also help youth make personal decisions about how they would prefer to act.

Conflicting School and Activity Schedules

More and more, American communities are scheduling youth activities at the hours that are traditionally left for the church and the Sunday school. This can mean real conflicts for youth. It can also be a major stumbling block for trying to recruit visitors and new members to the Sunday school classes.

Solution: Help teenagers recognize that such conflicts are common for those making Christian lifestyle decisions. This could be a valuable gift to their growing understanding about what faith must mean in their lives. Sometimes the best way to deal with the block is to get the youth more actively committed to the Sunday school by having stronger programs for them at a younger age.

Lack of Meeting Area

Gone are the days when the Sunday school can expect teenagers to have their class in the boiler room or the kitchen or some storage room. When youth feel left out or shoved off into a corner, they conclude that they are not important nor is their participation in Sunday school valuable. Almost every school district provides the finest furniture, quality equipment, and the most current resources for youth to have the finest educational experience. They are not used to hand-me-downs and are discouraged from full participation in a church that only gives them the leftovers.

Solution: Invite the young people to express their opinions about their classroom and its furniture and equipment. Seek suggestions on how they might solve the problems that they see. This involvement could help them to feel more ownership of their area, and they can even invent some very creative solutions to what they perceive as problems. Youth also need to assume the responsibility of living in a church that has dwindling resources in an affluent society.

Conflict Between Adult and Youth Values

Sometimes the idealism of youth in the church shakes the foundations and traditions of the adult members of the church. When this happens it is possible for a kind of tug-of-war to develop between youth and adults in the church. If this is allowed to continue, the youth are apt to give up on the church and will begin to drop out.

Solution: Do everything you can to avoid competition over time and space between groups in the church. Plan to use lots of intergenerational programs that require youth to participate, even to plan and lead.

Family Stress

Most parents feel that they lose contact (or control) over their children when they enter adolescence. Their child claims that the parents "don't know anything and can't really understand me." Some parents even feel that their teenager has become so self-centered that he or she has no concern whatsoever about what goes on in the rest of the family. (This is not really true; studies have shown over and again that parents and families still have more influence over teenagers than any other factor, including personal friends or peer pressure.) Such family stress can also have an impact on the church school participation of youth.

Solution: The effective Sunday school teacher knows the students well enough to know when stress in the family affects the youth. Strong personal relationships between teacher and young people can be very affirming when it helps them in such difficult times and encourages them to remain active in attending church school.

Change of Peer Relationships

It is always a great impetus to attendance for the boys in the Sunday school class to bring along their girlfriends; it works the same for girls. In the same way, if there has been a great deal of dating between members of the class, the break-up of a steady relationship can greatly affect the attendance patterns.

Solution: The teacher should keep contact with both parties involved in separation or conflict. They all can talk through feelings toward each other and how they feel about attending while their former "steady" is still there. This same principle ought to apply in the church when there is a divorce between active adult members of the church and one person feels he or she must leave the congregation if the spouse remains.

Note that the climate of relationships within the larger congregation is usually repeated in the youth. If there are a lot of conflicts between adult members of the church, similar conflicts will begin to show up between the teenagers in the Sunday school class. If the quality of relationships in the church family is one of reconciliation, mutual support, and care, that same kind of climate is likely to develop within the Sunday school class.

Stumbling blocks such as those listed above can make increasing attendance more difficult. But the best cure is often early prevention. Helping youth understand how their own stress can influence their church school attendance may be a wonderful preventive. It is well documented that one of the best ways to increase attendance is to prevent those who now attend from becoming dropouts.

Conclusion

As the Sunday school looks to its future, it is helpful to remember that there are fewer teenagers in the population today; those who are of teenage years between 1985 and 1995 are the smallest portion or percentage of our general population. In other words, there are far fewer teenagers per 1,000 people in this country than there are preschoolers, or, for that matter, those who are seventy years old and above. This fact alone accounts for some of the small attendance figures for teenagers in our churches in recent years. But in the next few years those figures will change and there will be more youth of this age in our society.

The other social factor for low attendance is that parents of those who are teenagers now were themselves passing out of adolescence during the 1960s, when a major part of our population chose not to be a part of any institution—church, fraternal, or other. Today's parents of teenagers may not have been in the church during their own adolescence. If we prepare ourselves and if we are conscientious as we reach out to youth, the rewards are likely to be very great. Let us not "despise our youth" because we think the case is hopeless. Instead, let us seek to call them effectively into full discipleship through our church schools.

8

The Young Adult

So then you are no longer strangers and sojourners, but you are fellow citizens with the saints and members of the household of God.

—Ephesians 2:19

Growing, healthy, vital churches practice a balanced ministry. They devote equal attention to evangelism, to meeting human physical needs and to socio-political action. God works through people. Therefore, evangelism is the launch pad for other ministries. If it doesn't work, nothing else will.

—Herb Miller[1]

One of the most difficult challenges for the ministry of Christian education is the recruitment and assimilation of young adults into the Sunday school. Today there is sufficient new evidence to suggest that the Sunday school should have higher expectations for bringing the young adult into the church. Opinion polls have shown there is a growing appetite in today's young adult for belief in God and a desire for greater understanding of a personal faith.[2]

Young adults have been given more attention and been the object of more research than any other group in the 1980s. Religious organizations have been trying to analyze the attitudes and developmental needs of this large population group. "Baby boomers" have been the target of much investigation by sociologists, psychologists, political parties, employers, and advertisers. All this data has shown that the young adults are more interested in the church than they have been at any time in the last three decades.

111

The baby boom generation is usually counted as those persons who were born between 1946 and 1965. The peak birth year of that group was 1957.

The Lutheran Church in America examined "The Baby Boom Generation in Congregations of the Lutheran Church in America" through a special research project in 1986.[3] This project identified several specific characteristics that describe the young adult. These include: (a) high levels of energy, enthusiasm, and creativity; (b) openness to new ideas, new challenges; (c) a readiness for involvement, commitment, and willingness to assume responsibility for groups to which they belong; and (d) competence in leadership capabilities and a desire for the opportunity to apply their creativity.

Several key issues or themes seem to dominate the concerns or thinking of the baby boomers: family, sexuality, and children; job and vocational questions; ethical questions related to daily life; and personal faith and spiritual meaning in life.

The Alban Institute targeted this group for extensive research in recent years, and it also found that many young adults are returning to the church.[4] Much to the surprise of church leaders, they are returning with a more conservative theological and political stance; and they are returning to the church at an age much younger than is usually associated with this age group. The commonly held belief has been that young adults return at about ages thirty to forty when their children are beginning to start preschool. In the 1980s the average age of young adults returning to the church was twenty-six to thirty six.

One United Church of Christ study discovered that those young adults who do attend church have increased their regular attendance patterns; in 1984, 42.8 percent were attending worship at least three times per month, while in 1972-74 only 33.5 percent reported this attendance level. The study also found that this age group has definite ideas about what it wants from the church, the major focus of which is spirituality, family life, and community concern.[5]

It is important to understand that this segment of the population is not one uniform group. Many churches have made a meager attempt at programming for a new group of singles or young adults and have been very disappointed in the results. One major cause of the failure is the assumption that most people between the ages of eighteen and forty have pretty much the same interests and lifestyle.

Bob Gribbon of the Alban Institute has been very helpful in describing three subgroups:[6]

Transitional Young Adults. The eighteen-to twenty-five-year olds are often moving away from home. They need a ministry that encourages independence and that supports them in their transition. Most persons in this group are single and are pursuing their drive to enter the work force. For many this involves college. This group has come to its adulthood since the rapid growth of personal computers and the revolution in the media brought about by the videocasette recorder, satellite transmission, and cable networks.

Young Adults in Their Twenties. For the most part these young adults are beginning to establish their first homes and their own independent value system. Some are beginning to marry and later to start child rearing. For singles, as well as for those who are married, the primary concern is progress in a career. Many women in this age group have delayed childbearing much later than have the generations before them. This age group came to its maturity after the Vietnam war era, after Watergate and the first resignation of a U.S. President.

Young Adults in Their Thirties. For most of this group the primary agenda is starting families, going to P.T.A. meetings and Scout groups, and purchasing their first homes; others have already experienced their first divorce. This is the post-Woodstock generation, when most of the impact of the civil rights movement, the anti-war generation, and the Beatles mania was already past. For this older group of young adults the primary life issue is the need to gain comfort and confidence in intimate relationships. As they approach the traditional age of mid-life reassessment, they flounder for a sense of values. Since they often rejected much of society's demand for rigid moral guidelines and resisted the power and influence of institutions, there are few sources of guidance in their spiritual quest.

Characteristics of Young Adults

—Among the young adults in this decade, a new work force in the middle class has emerged, quite different from the "blue collar" workers of their parents' generation. Because most young adults are substantially better educated than their parents, they have become accountants, teachers, nurses, salespersons, computer programmers, and lab technicians—that is, they are employed in the service industry of our economy. Ralph Whitehead, a University of Massachusetts demographer and political strategist has labeled these young adults "New Collar Workers."[7]

New Collar Workers are not the indifferent "Yuppies" that have been the focus of so much popular analysis. The New Collar Workers are members of parents' organizations, Scout leaders, and elected community servants. As a group they are most likely to seek out, to attend, and to join our churches and church schools.

—Unlike the young adults in the late 1950s and most of the 1960s, this group is not so apt to reject society's restrictive mores and to oppose institutions. Many of those perceived restraints have already been removed for today's young adults and they do not wish to be liberated from the restraints that currently exist. They yearn for a more moderate lifestyle and are concerned about their own place in society rather than about society's restrictions on them. Young adults today appreciate strong, conservative moral values and equality of opinion. Most are seeking some spiritual meaning in their personal pilgrimage.

Those who are not a part of the institutional church assume that most current members of the church are intolerant of the moral freedom and lifestyle that most young adults seek. In fact, they may not be aware that the mainline Protestant church was probably the champion of the personal freedom and lifestyle they now enjoy.

—According to the 1986 survey of young adults conducted by the Lutheran Church in America, there is a set of general characteristics of the baby boom generation that tends to discourage the young adult from taking the initiative to begin attending Sunday school.

1. They tend to be self-centered and self-absorbed.
2. They have very busy schedules.
3. Many practice non-traditional lifestyles.
4. Many are financially over-extended.
5. Most are resistant to making long-term commitments.
6. They usually see the church as "irrelevant" until children arrive.
7. They have great mobility.
8. There is much competition for their time and money.
9. If they attend any church, their attendance is apt to be very irregular—especially for singles.
10. There is a great diversity among these young adults, and their personal needs are quite varied.[8]

In order for any church school to plan for and attract this group of adults, it must clearly seek to address the ongoing life concerns of these persons. In many ways the ministry of Christian education is best equipped to offer for these adults what they need most in their lives.

The Kinds of Education These Adults Prefer

Programs that help people grow spiritually. Young adults are seeking programs that help people discover life's meaning. For many this is best done in caring, supportive fellowship and study groups rather than traditional lecture-dominated classes. Courses or topics must be relevant to their own real-life concerns.

Do not assume that these life concerns focus primarily on ethical or moral issues in our society. That was the agenda for the young adult two decades ago. Today's life concerns include an appetite to learn more about themselves, about the Bible, and about ways to enhance their lives through their spiritual journey.

Lyle Schaller has made the helpful observation that many who are looking for a church home today are looking for a waystation on their life pilgrimage and not necessarily a permanent home.[9] There is not as much allegiance to the denomination one belonged to as a child. Young adults are looking for the church that meets their current needs.

A strong sense of belonging. Young adults want to be welcomed into a church where they feel connected. They need to be part of a group where they are able to make a difference in their world because their efforts are combined with others who have similar concerns. They are aware that the world is filled with hungry, homeless millions, that it is characterized by injustice and oppression, both social and political.

In his book *30 Year Olds and the Church,* R.T. Gribbon suggests that what they mostly look for in a church are: "Place, pastor, program and people." In response to the question, "Why did you join this church?" most responded, "I liked the people."[10]

Focus on the family. Young adults respond best to a church that strengthens family life while also being open to young people who are single or are living together in various forms of family commitments.

The fellowship of a Sunday school group can serve as the extended family for many young adults. This is especially needed in a mobile society.

Quality programs. This generation of adults demands "quality" in the programs of the church. They are substantially better educated than former generations. They have grown up with television and some of its sophistocated programming. They are used to having lots of choices in their everyday lives, whether for products, housing, or community resources. So they expect to see high quality in the buildings, the programs, and the leadership of the church.

Some studies have shown that young adults may be more drawn to larger congregations because they assume there are greater resources for quality of worship services and music, more competent preaching, more programs, and more options for their children, etc.

Strong children's programs. Young adults are seeking religious and moral training for their children. This means clean and attractive nurseries as well as outstanding classes for all children. Single parents especially need reasonable child care for them to be able to participate fully in the programs of the church and to serve as volunteers in leadership positions. A single parent has real difficulty accepting an appointment to the church's boards or councils when they also have to pay for child care during the meetings.

Access to leadership. Young adults expect women and other minorities to have equal access to the leadership and decision-making in the church. The church currently is lagging behind compared to most other institutions in our society. Young adults today are well qualified to assume leadership roles in the church and may resent not being able to donate their skills.

Stepping Stones to Increased Attendance

1. Keep attendance records. Not only is it important to keep some record of the regular members and how often they attend, it is essential to record the names and addresses of each visitor or prospect. These prospects can be paired with members who are to follow up immediately after a person visits for the first time.

Remember that a Sunday morning Sunday school is not the only occasion when young adults can be in church learning groups. It is helpful to keep attendance records of these other learning events. Especially note the total number of different persons who attend.

2. *Offer different teaching/learning styles.* On some occasions young adults prefer a qualified expert to teach a subject about which they have little experience or knowledge. On other subjects, which are more experiential in content, they prefer lots of opportunity for open discussion on the subject, and they expect to share leadership.

3. *Offer new classes.* Be sure there are strong leaders for these courses. Groups or classes that have been together more than three years begin having more and more difficulty assimilating new members. New classes are more open to new members.

Young adults are often reluctant to commit themselves to long-term membership in a class, so a variety of short-term courses may be a valuable alternative.

4. *Include child care and nursery services for all events.* Remember that very young children do not do well in a nursery for long periods of time. Adult programs should be scheduled to last no longer than the endurance of the children for whom care is being provided..

5. *Provide varied activities.* These must cover a broad spectrum of interests, such as parties, sports programs, study groups, personal enrichment events, and service projects to the community.

6. *Provide attractive classrooms.* Be sure that all meeting places for young adults are clean and attractive.

7. *Include lots of food and fellowship in the programs that include young adults.* In many settings these must also meet today's current "healthful" restrictions.

8. *Teach people how to feel comfortable while describing to the unchurched what their faith means to them.* Help young adults overcome their "evangelphobia."[11] Help them learn to say why attending your church is an important part of their lives.

9. *Use special events or short course offerings for inviting new visitors to your church.* One of the best events is a Christmas Eve service designed for families of young children. A midnight service will have more appeal to singles and the younger adults without children. Vacation church school is a good program to make contact with new young families.

10. *Utilize the gifts and skills of these newcomers in the mission of the church.* Too often we wait for newcomers to be

trained by the church to do the traditional church jobs. Most Sunday schools need to learn how to include new members in the leadership of the church much sooner than they have in the past.

11. Train newcomers to reach out to invite prospects for the church school who are currently unchurched. Most people choose to visit or join a church because they were invited by a friend or family member. Newcomers have a whole new network of unchurched friends that can be prospects for your church school.

12. Provide church events that are designed to include the whole family with multiple generations. For many young adults, especially singles or families whose extended families live in other cities, the church school can become a substitute family. The groups in the church school can serve as their support network in a difficult and fast-paced world.

13. See that programs are conducted with enthusiasm and joy. The church must not be controlled by a feeling of discouragement or depression if it ever expects to grow. Today's young adults have too many options to put up with a place where they have to generate enthusiasm or have to work hard to find enjoyment.

14. Help young adults face the transitions in their lives. This can be done with seminars or with resources. It can be done by offering friendship and sharing advice. Some examples of the most common points of transition for young adults are:

Marriage	Divorce
Making a move	New employment or promotion
Loss of employment	Birth of the first child
Child enters first grade	Death of a parent
Major health crisis	Health crisis of parents

15. Begin groups for women. Because young adult women are rarely assimilated well into the existing women's organizations, the church school can be the best place to involve young women in the church. Programs for single career women can be helpful. Support groups may be provided for recently widowed, for those sexually abused, for single parents, and for those entering the work force for the first time.

The fifteen ideas—stepping stones—listed above are only a few suggestions that can help the Sunday school experience growth in the attendance of young adults.

Overcoming Stumbling Blocks

The traditional congregation can set up a number of roadblocks to growth in church school attendance of the young adult:

Assuming there is only one kind of family

It can be a real "turn-off" to young adults if the church they visit constantly talks about the family and clearly intends to mean only the families who have a papa and mama and 2.3 children. There are many new family configurations in our society today: We have single parents with children, formerly married friends sharing homes, singles, young married adults who have no children and who do not plan to have any. For so many years the church school seemed to have such a limited view of the family that many young adults felt the Sunday school was judgmental of their lifestyle if it was other than a traditional family.

Solution: This is, first of all, an issue of consciousness. The best thing the church school can do is help the congregation appreciate the many kinds of family configurations that exist. It might even be helpful to avoid the word family for most church gatherings. Plan intergenerational events so that childless families can become acquainted with children in the church. Some churches even encourage older adults and single adults to "adopt" some of the children in the Sunday school as substitute aunts and uncles.

Scheduling events at only one time of the week

Today's lifestyle for many single and childless young adults discourages attendance at early Sunday morning classes. Those who work with singles will also testify to the fact they they resist commitment to attend consistently any group or program.

Solution: Offer short-term elective courses, or more retreat or weekend events. For some mothers with preschool children, a weekday morning class might be best. For other professional young adults, a weekday morning breakfast meeting may be the answer.

Avoiding discussion of personal hurts or problems

Any Sunday school that avoids discussing personal issues and real life hurts will be seen as "superficial" to the true seeker of spiritual meaning in life. This same attitude will prevail if the church is unwilling to question its own church doctrine. While teachers must be confident in the validity of their own beliefs, they must not be judgmental about new religious concepts.

Solution: Teach the Bible! The more a Sunday school can pass on the old old story, the more young adults will be able to adopt its message as directive of their own story. Plan for and provide the kind of settings and groups where the climate of trust and comfort can develop.

Neglect of the nursery and other building needs

Over the past two decades some churches decided to spend more of their church's income for charitable causes beyond their congregation—for hunger, for outreach, for mission, and for social justice movements—than for the congregation's comfort or beauty. For some very appropriate and even laudable reasons the church and Christian education buildings were allowed to decline. Many church school facilities may appear outdated, the paint may be peeling, and there may be lots of broken chairs and equipment.

Today these conditions will not speak to visitors of commitment to serve others rather than ourselves. They will represent neglect, lack of interest, apathy, or even disregard for the importance of Christian learning for either children or adults. The message of concern for others will be lost on today's young adults, who will expect to find quality facilities and quality programs.

Solution: Throw away unnecessary and outdated furniture. Have a paint-up day. Select a room or department or section of your building each year to "renovate." Have fund raisers to assist in updating specific areas. This will show the church school's commitment to quality and excellence, even though it is not possible to solve all the building problems at once.

Move some classes to more attractive and comfortable spaces in the building. Do not select only leftover spaces like the kitchen for young adults. Actually, middle and recently retired adults have more tolerance for such accommodations than do newcomer young adults.

Your church can unknowingly set up these common stumbling blocks that prevent the attendance of young adults. But they can be handled when persons are aware of their presence and try new solutions to eliminate their power.

Conclusion

In the next decade the church school can expect to see more growth in this age group of adults than in any other. Many are dusting off old cribs for the nursery because there are new babies coming along. Sadly, most churches do not really perceive this as true growth; they are apt to think it is only some kind of an unusual situation that is not likely to last. This judgment, in turn, prevents them from building upon the momentum that is already present.

If the Sunday school can change its expectations, be more optimistic and therefore be more active in changing what it does in the church school for the young adult, there is substantial reason to believe that it can and should grow. Until we invite new persons to join us in the Sunday school, those persons will have no real opportunity to learn about the good news for their lives.

9

Middle Adults

". . . at the time for the banquet he sent his servant to say to those who had been invited, 'Come; for all is now ready.' . . . The first said to him, 'I have bought a field and I must go out and see it. . . . 'And another said, 'I have bought five yoke of oxen, and I go to examine them. . . . ' And another said, 'I have married a wife, and therefore I cannot come.'"

—Luke 14:17-25

"[People] are seeking a church that can respond effectively to the needs they encounter on their personal and spiritual journey in life. This often means the church with a strong evangelistic thrust must strengthen its adult ministries."

—Lyle Schaller[1]

Adults who have reached the middle years, ages thirty-five to sixty, are traditionally the most active participants in the Sunday school. We rely heavily on this group to be teachers and advisers in the children's and youth classes, leaders responsible for administering the program of Christian education. Yet over the past few years there has been a growing sense of frustration in many churches because we have not been able to increase the attendance and participation of this age group in the church school.

Authors of church growth principles think this is the most important group to attract to the Sunday school because they bring their children. We have not been very effective at attracting more adults in this age group into our Sunday schools in recent years.

This group of adults is also the most active in the leadership of all areas of church life. Compared to the 1950s and the 1960s, a much smaller percentage of this age group is now active in the church. There are basically two reasons for this: (1) there are fewer adults in this group than any other age cohort; and (2) this group, especially the younger portion, rejected the influence of institutions in our society and chose not to return to church when their children were small as had so many adults before and since.

These members have the freshest memories of the struggles over the radical changes in social, political, and moral values in the 1960s and 70s. They may be convinced that several of their friends were divorced because of what they call the "women's lib" movement. Their children are apt to have been the radical "anti-war," "anti-family," "anti-morals," and "anti-church" generation. Some men in this age group may be feeling that their careers and chances for job advancement were jeopardized by affirmative action.

Those who are still a part of the church and its Sunday school may feel they are the "faithful few." They are discouraged and believe that there is no reason to think that there could be any growth in the Sunday school. They are more apt to talk about "meaningful" religious education than they are to advocate new methods for increasing attendance.

The youngest of this group (ages thirty-five to forty-five) make up the first part of the great baby boom following World War II. They came of age in the 1950s with all its optimism and freedom. Most purchased their homes some years ago and spend only a small percentage of their disposable income for house payments.

This group grew up in the church during the "golden age of the Sunday school." In those days people were joining the church in great numbers. People not only were joining Sunday schools, they were joining Scout troops, Kiwanis, Lions clubs, and many other social groups. Most churches were building new education buildings, with separate classrooms for each age level of children. Sunday school growth seemed almost inevitable in the suburbs.

The second group (ages forty-six to fifty-five) grew up during World War II and the Korean War. They are very likely to have attended church as a child or adolescent. In those years, church school did not have to compete with television, athletic programs, or even school events. Many communities had a common understanding that Wednesday was always "church night." For these adults the church youth group was often the center of their social lives.

For most people in this age sector or older, the only roles they saw men assume in the Sunday school were those of the superintendent (or clerk), the chair of the department or council of Christian education, or the teachers of an adult class. Some may have been advisers to the youth group or served as leaders of the scouting programs. Men did not expect to teach younger children unless their denomination separated the boys from the girls in the earlier classes. Most men in this age group were more apt to serve in leadership positions outside the territory of the Sunday school.

The older portion of this group of middle adults (ages fifty-five to sixty-five) grew up during the Great Depression, so that most of their understanding of the proper role of an adult in society is shaped by the need for financial security for themselves and their families. The church they knew probably did not have graded programs for all ages of children and adults, so that few can recall attending church school until they were adolescents or even young adults.

These middle adults who are in the Sunday school today are very likely to have been active for twenty or thirty years. Most of those years have seen the church and the Sunday school continue to decline despite their best human efforts. Some are even resentful that they are the "only" faithful Christians because they believe that most other middle adults have abandoned the church.

For these reasons they tend to be tenaciously loyal to the church. For many this loyalty extends to a particular denomination as well. They compare their church with other denominations and feel they are in competition for a limited pool of middle adults.

Yet there are reasons to be encouraged about increasing the attendance of middle-aged adults in church school. The stepping stones in this chapter will help the church make some progress in this age group. Let us first look at the characteristics of middle adults so we can better address their personal life concerns to provide a religious education that will have meaning and lasting effect in their everyday living.

Roadsigns for Understanding Middle Adults

—Most of this group were trained in one profession that they assumed they would pursue all their lives, and that, once they were married and had a home and two children, they would have reached that mystical status of mature adults. Now, however, some are experiencing what is being called "middlescence," when they reassess their personal identity and whether they can still find enjoyment and challenge in their vocations. For many women the choice was to be home-maker and nurturing parent. Now, with children moving off to college, they may need a new sense of self-worth. For many men, it may be a matter of coming to grips with unfulfilled dreams.

—This age group has a strong need to be in control of their lives while at the same time they are deeply committed to fulfilling their obligations as parents. Many feel a new responsibility of caring for their own aging parents.

—This group assumes a lot of responsibility in the leadership of their community (service clubs and political or community organizations) as well as the church.

—Most of the adults in this age group have been active members of the church for a long time. They have partici-pated in a wide variety of learning programs in the church. They feel the church is a place where they meet their closest friends and greatly enjoy the fellowship.

—This group is usually more financially secure and has more choices about how to spend their leisure time than any group before them. Yet they can readily understand the people in the parable of Jesus in which the master planned a special banquet and invited many friends. Most of the friends were too busy (buying new land, getting married, buying a new set of oxen, or burying a father) to be able to attend. Middle adults often have to send their regrets to invitations because they are too busy to work it into their schedule.

The Kinds of Education These Adults Prefer

Lots of fellowship. They enjoy opportunities for fellowship and getting to know personally the other adults in a group. They usually feel that there is little value in a church event unless there is a large group attending, and they express disappointment if attendance is low.

Focus on the Bible. They have a strong appetite to grow in their understanding of the Bible and how it informs their everyday personal lives. Some adult groups prefer to study a current bestseller about self-esteem, spiritual growth, or social issues rather than a specific study on Bible facts. Still, they want to apply their learning in a way that is appropriate for a Christian.

A broad choice of topics. The church must regularly be offering new topics and new groups for the unchurched middle adults. Some would prefer to have a group to belong to, while others prefer short elective courses that require only a limited time commitment.

A discussion format and shared leadership. Most such study groups share leadership, with each person taking a turn rather than one outstanding teacher who will always be the leader. They usually prefer a discussion method over a lecture.

Stepping Stones to Church School Growth

1. Keep accurate records. It is always important to have names, addresses, and telephone numbers in order to publicize new programs and all social affairs for each adult class.

One church school encourages its class teachers or leaders in every group to spend some time in each class session noting those who are absent and asking if any class members have news about absentees. They encourage class members to volunteer to contact the missing members to express support or concern.

Most small churches are apt to feel that such record keeping is truly unnecessary. However, (a) it reminds everyone that regular and consistent attendance is important and valuable, and (b) it makes it easier to get the names, addresses, and telephone numbers of all visitors. Except in the very smallest rural communities, invitations to return to class or to attend a social function of the class or other church celebration, are best extended by telephone or mail. It is easy for newcomers to forget the exact time and place for such special events; a written notice helps them keep the facts straight.

2. Encourage lots of fellowship. Plan for your current classes to find more occasions for getting acquainted, for sharing life stories, and for having fun together. For many middle-adult church school classrooms, a standard piece of equipment is a functioning coffee pot. This announces that class members expect to spend some time catching up on each other's news.

Regular parties are also helpful to middle adults. Variety in these social events throughout a year's time will help each class member feel his or her interests are being met. For some, an active event like a picnic with a softball game is just the thing; for others, an evening of board games is special; for others, it may be a trip to a drama performance; and for others, cooking an international dinner together.

3. *Offer Bible study classes that emphasize life concerns as well as the devotional meaning for personal life.* There are generally four approaches to the selection of curriculum resources for this age group.

a. Denominational curriculum and/or Uniform Lesson Series.

b. The pastor, or a well educated leader, designs a special course either on a particular book of the Bible, a certain Bible author, or on one topic, such as faith, forgiveness, etc.

c. Independently published study guides from well known authors, utilizing videotapes and other types of study resources.

d. A specially-designed intensive study program for adults: The most popular seem to be "The Trinity Bible Series," "Kerygma," "Bethel Bible Series," and "A.B.I.L."

For some churches these approaches are best done in regular continuing classes on Sunday morning. For others, it could mean starting a new group or meeting at another time, such as Sunday evening. Meeting at other times could be a way of including all those other middle adults who are too busy during Sunday morning with other responsibilities: teaching children's classes, being Sunday school superintendent, singing in choir, and the like.

4. *Offer short-term elective topical courses.* Offer a changing set of topics from which adults can choose, including some that might open new doors for prospects who are attracted by a special topic. Such topics might be: Divorce Recovery, Helping a Friend Through Grief, A Christian Approach to Depression, Sending Your Child Off to College for the First Time.

5. *Start new classes.* Provide a variety of teaching methods so adults can make choices. Some of the prospects for beginning a new permanent class could be those who have attended one of the elective courses.

6. *Identify prospects to invite to class.* Current class members probably will need help to identify prospects. This age group of adults usually needs to broaden its perspective of who to invite to Sunday school. Most middle-aged adults who have been active in the church have few friends they have not already invited. So they assume they know no one who might be a prospect.

Class members could find prospects among new employees in

the company for which they work, new persons who have moved into the community, someone who has lived through a difficult divorce and feels uncomfortable about attending his or her former church, the person who cuts or styles their hair, the new schoolteacher that moved into town, the volunteer who works with them in Scouts, the auxiliary of the hospital, or someone who sings next to them in the community choir or plays on the same softball or bowling league. Other prospects are even members of their families, such as a spouse, a new sister-in-law, a parent who has come to live with them.

7. *Teach middle adults how to talk invitingly about their church school.* Most middle adults in the mainline churches have a great fear of evangelism because of their assumptions about its demands for personal witnessing. Their image is of some powerful preacher who comes to visit their church from out of town, or the radical nuisance who is always talking about "the Lord" at the most inappropriate occasion. They dread that they might have to act that same way. Many think they can not invite a visitor to Sunday school because they feel they will not know what to say. Still others think they have not been members of their particular parish or denomination long enough to represent the church well—they worry they might say the wrong thing. We need to teach adults how to invite prospects to church, to reach out to the unchurched.

Newcomers are often the best equipped to invite other visitors because they are usually more conscious of the primary reasons that attracted them to Sunday school and led them to become regular members. They need assistance to articulate those reasons and to invite other prospective members.

8. *Help people through their life transitions.* This stepping stone to increasing church school attendance is one that communicates Christian love and concern. People who are coming back to church school in the 1990s are looking for a place where their personal and spiritual needs will be met. They personally experience such love and concern when they see others being cared for by the church school.

Caring for middle adults in the church school is also a way to keep those who are now attending from becoming dropouts. Sunday school members are most at risk of dropping out when there has been a death in their family, when they are going through a health crisis or divorce, when their teenage children get in trouble, when they lose their jobs or are demoted (or even passed over for promotion), or when there is conflict in the church. If the church school can help people through these crises and help them remain in the class, they will also be great ambassadors for the church.

Overcoming Stumbling Blocks

There are several common blocks to growth in church school attendance; some are particularly related to adults in this middle-aged group.

Resistance to Change

It may seem ironic that these adults, who were often the initiators of significant changes in the church school, are now apt to be the most resistant to further changes. Two explanations may account for such a fear of change: (1) middle adults have experienced so many life transitions in the normal course of events that they have a strong personal need to find stability and predictability in their churches; (2) many of the changes needed in the Sunday school now may appear to reverse a former change for which these adults struggled earlier. Once a difficult decision has been made, especially one that affects the whole church and includes a lot of controversy, adults are strongly invested in the status quo and find it very difficult to resurrect the same subject a second time—even if a whole generation has passed since the first debate.

Sometimes this fear of change translates itself into a reluctance to let newcomers share the decision-making and leadership roles. The influx of newcomers may create an entirely new and different climate. Middle adults who have been members a long time sometimes resent these "Johnny-come-latelies" because they were not there during the period of decline and did not help wage the battles for survival of ten and twenty years ago.

Solution: Provide lots of ministries of fellowship and support. When adults feel that their concerns have been heard, that they are valued, and that someone else will look out for their concerns, they begin to lose their defensiveness and their fear of change. Since most middle adults assume responsibility for their children, for their spouses' happiness, for their parents' health and well being, and even for the future profits of their company, they are greatly relieved to be cared for and nurtured by others in the Sunday school.

Previous Conflicts in Church

Inasmuch as middle adults are often the most involved in the leadership of the church, they are also the most vulnerable to criticism and attacks on the leadership of the church. If the congregation is filled with controversy, it is difficult for newcomers to feel welcome. When newcomers visit, they may feel the tension that continues to exist between long-time members, or they may feel left out because they were not members when some former controversy occurred.

Solution: Start new groups of adults. When newcomers join others of the same experience, they begin their own history. It usually takes each new group some time before the members begin to really feel a deep attachment to one another, often as long as three years, so it is important when starting new groups not to keep pulling new members out of their group for service elsewhere. They need the time to develop relationships that will endure.

Low Expectations

We have talked before about this age group generally having the expectation that there are very few prospects for the church school. They assume there is little reason for hope that it can grow. They tried each new gimmick that was suggested through the years with little or no progress; their church school probably even experienced decline.

Solution: Recruit these leaders to attend area, conference, or district workshops and assemblies of the church. Here they can tell their war stories and hear the experiences of other churches. They may discover that they have been doing some very creative things in comparison to other congregations, and they will hear from others some exciting new ideas that they might use for themselves.

Resentments

For some middle adult groups there is resentment toward the church and toward newcomers; they are tired of so many years of hard work that has produced very little progress or growth. If this resentment displays itself in cynicism and pessimism, it can really dampen the spirit of any church school and discourage newcomers.

Solution: Find ways to celebrate the achievements of the past.

Give rewards and appreciation to the long-time members. Help middle adults appreciate the gifts given to them by their own early church school teachers of years ago. Let them, in turn, find joy in becoming spiritual mentors to newcomers and younger adults and children in your church. Also, help them recognize the gifts and insights of newcomers.

Lack of Space for New Classes

Since starting new classes is a primary method for increasing attendance in this age group, space can be a problem.

Solution: Change the schedule so that the same rooms or spaces can be used more than once. This may take some real ingenuity to avoid people feeling that their family group spirit is being broken up. If other groups meet at new and different times, be sure to count participants as Sunday school attenders so the education department or council knows that participation of newcomers has increased the attendance.

Too Few Roles for Men

The traditional roles for men in the church are usually limited to positions as chairs of committees or teachers of adult classes. Most of these positions require a style of leadership that depends heavily on the ability to express oneself in large groups. The church school therefore is best able to include and utilize men who are lawyers, teachers, salesmen, authors, managers, etc. There are not as many roles for men who are uncomfortable with speaking in public or expressing their opinions in groups. Men who are left out of the church are mechanics, barbers, factory workers, farmers—those who find their vocation in the work of their hands and not in their ability to speak. This limiting of places for full participation in the church discourages growth.

Women also find their roles in the church limiting. However, the church school has traditionally found more places for service and for achievement by women than for men. Middle-aged women can find more entrances into groups of the Sunday school than can men.

Solution: Encourage more groups to include fellowship as a central part of their experience. Encourage each class to do more service projects that utilize skills other than speaking. Men can build playground equipment for the preschool; they can pick up shut-ins and bring them to church; they can cook a special breakfast on Mother's Day or Scout Sunday, operate a food booth at a local county or crafts fair, or make new signs for the church.

Conclusion

A great deal can be done to increase the attendance of middle adults. More than any other age level, this one will require church school leaders to adopt new ways of thinking and new ideas in order for this growth to occur.

10

Older Adults

"So even to old age and gray hairs,
O God, do not forsake me,
till I proclaim thy might
to all the generations to come."

—Psalm 71:18

"True evangelism works patiently and lovingly to keep the
Christian experience a growing experience in the life of [each]
person."

—Mildred Parker[1]

At this time in history the population of older adults is one of the most fertile soils for the church's evangelism efforts and for the growth of the Sunday school. Not only are there more older adults now in our population than ever before, they are living longer, they are in more vigorous health, and they are more financially secure than at any other time.

Yet, the church school is more guilty of neglecting older adults than any other age. We do not expect increased attendance in older adults after age sixty-five. Either their classes are stable with very loyal attendance, or they are beginning to decline through home confinement and death. We believe that "old folks are too set in their ways" to want to change and begin coming to Sunday school.

One common myth is expressed like this: "It is sad that our congregation is mostly made up of old folks." Or, more often, we hear it stated as: "If this church doesn't bring in some new young families we are going to die." No one seems to recognize that this implies older adults no longer need spiritual nurture and evangelization. We act as if we have written off anyone over sixty-five from the Sunday school.

Some authors have suggested that younger and middle-aged adults are the only proper targets for church growth efforts. These authors assume that: (a) parents, not children, make the decisions about whether or not they can attend Sunday school, and (b) older adults have stopped deciding about their spiritual lives. That attitude is an uninformed and judgmental one; it assumes there are few opportunities for ministry to older adults.

By contrast, Lyle Schaller suggests that there are some parts of the country, especially new growing retirement communities, where older adults are the most productive group to target for church school growth.[2]

The principles that produce growing church schools apply to the older adult population as well as to any other generation; two in particular are: (a) people are most open to consider church membership and issues of personal faith when life changes or crises provoke them to raise questions of the meaning of life; and (b) people are most likely to come to the church school because of an invitation by a church member who knows the prospect through kinship or social contact networks.

The former principle applies to older adults at retirement, moving to a new apartment, moving to live closer to children, death of a spouse, declining health, death of close friends, etc. The latter principle addresses older persons' need for companionship and fellowship as their circle of friendships begins to decline with the aging and death of friends.

A great deal of attention and study has been devoted to older adults in our society in recent years. The church has discussed some of the ways it needs to minister to older adults, but little has been published about their needs for learning more about faith—namely through Christian education. Let us look at their personal needs and consider what kind of church school ministry is most appropriate for persons in this age group.

What About Older Adults?

—Most all adults are living longer. They can be active volunteer leaders in the church much longer than their parents before them. Each congregation has a longer list of shut-in members because medical care for the elderly is better. They are reaching the time of retirement much healthier than ever before. Most churches are governed by these "elders." We depend upon this service. Yet changing life situations may make it helpful for them to accept shorter terms of office or to have two persons share a year's responsibility.

—As older adults mature and retire, when they have more time for friends, their circle of friends may become smaller. Those who have been active in the church all those years are apt to have few friends who are not already in the church. In today's society there is a great likelihood that their children and grandchildren do not live in the same community.

—They have more financial resources than any generation before them. Some analysts predict that their own children will not have the same financial resources in retirement that this generation of older adults enjoy. This age group provides the bulk of the financial support for the church.

Yet because many grew up or were already adults during the depression years, they have a fear of dwindling resources. They are always saving for the "rainy day," an attitude reinforced by the fear they could outlive their resources.

—Older adults today are better able to travel than any group before them. This is a result of financial resources and better health. There is a whole new group who live six months in the sunny South and six months in the temperate North. Others are able to make extended trips all around the globe.

Roadsigns for Understanding Older Adults

—Most older adults in the church are loyal. Older adult classes tend to have better attendance records than younger groups. They often feel they must be at every church function.

—Older adults experience a sense of loneliness as friends move away or transfer to nursing homes and as spouses die. The need for companionship is often met by being active in church affairs. There is a fear that with aging one will not remain independent and self-sufficient. This fear and loneliness often provoke depression in aging older adults.

—Older adults have a strong need to know that their lives have "counted for something." They want to share their stories, their values, and their wisdom with younger persons. Older adults will often use their free time to serve as volunteers.

—The time of retirement can be a very difficult time. Many people have not really planned or accepted retirement; they feel that society has locked them out of the world of productivity, which provides a sense of personal worth. The percentage of males who die between the ages of sixty-five and sixty-seven jumps dramatically. It is not because their bodies fall apart at that time but because their spirits die.

—Some older adults (depending on the individual) have a great appetite to learn, a strong curiosity. Many take courses at community colleges, hear lectures at their clubs, and plan vacations with Elderhostel programs.

There are as many biological and social changes between sixty and eighty as there are between birth and twenty. Some authorities suggest that people go through more psychological changes in the last twenty years of their lives than they do in the first sixty. Retirement; death of friends, spouses, and children; lack of income; failing health; reduced mobility—all of these are traumatic for the older person.[3]

It is important to remember that older adults are as varied as any other group in the population. They do not all think alike, nor do they have the same lifestyle or religious faith.

Educational Implications for Older Adults

Use the lecture/discussion method. Older adults have years of experience at learning this way and usually prefer this style for their learning at church.

Use travel as a teaching method, even field trips in the city. Neither older adults nor the church usually recognize that travel is a learning method useful for this age group.

Use the Bible as the main content. There is usually a great yearning to know the Bible better.

Provide time for fellowship. Such fellowship is important so that older adults feel they are needed and cherished. They love to spend many hours with friends at church. They find it enriching to take care of one another in times of crisis and need. They enjoy events where they can be around children also.

Let the older adults teach. They will share the stories of their own faith journeys and their values to a new generation.

Stepping Stones to Growth with Older Adults

There are several ways to begin to bring older adults into the church school and to generate greater attendance.

1. Keep attendance records. This allows for recognition of birthdates, anniversaries, and the like. Keep adequate records of names, addresses, birthdates, and names of close relatives who visit on occasion. This is helpful information during time of distress or illness.

Older adults need to know that the best prospects for the Sunday school are friends of present members who need a church home, or new persons who have moved into the community.

2. Rely on the lecture/discussion method. Older adults often prefer one teacher per class or two or three who share the leadership. The best teachers have clear speaking voices so that they are able to be heard.

For the youngest of this age group—the most recently retired—there is often a preference for shared leadership within the class, having each person take a turn as the leader.

3. Provide personal support during times of transition and stress. A Sunday school class that hopes to grow must have systems that keep it alert to each person, to provide sympathy at times of grief, to provide transportation when a spouse is in the hospital, and to show genuine caring and support. When older adults can speak with pride about the growth experience of support during hard times, they are great ambassadors for recruiting new members.

4. Provide adequate facilities for older adults. There are several specific needs for older adults to be comfortable in their classrooms and to get the most out of their learning experience.

—the classroom close to the entrance of the church
—convenient parking near that entrance

—large, clean bathrooms on the same floor as the classroom
—comfortable seating
—few stairs to get to classroom or to the sanctuary
—adequate lighting to be able to read their curriculum or Bibles
—large-print Bibles, curriculum, and devotional books
—wheelchairs and walkers (both to use during class and to be borrowed during times of ill health)

Another way to help older adults feel comfortable and feel included is to plan no night meetings, especially in bad weather. Fridays and Saturdays are often used by grandparents to visit with children, so they are not good times for fellowship or field trips. The growing church school class will need to have a network to provide transportation for the class time or for other functions.

5. *Start new social programs.* Find out what new programs might be started for the adults who are not now part of the church program. Special elective classes might focus on such topics as: understanding Social Security and Medicare changes, writing wills, planning for investments, preventing crimes, developing one's spiritual side. Other classes might teach new crafts or writing skills, introduce new hobbies, or provide travel lectures and book reviews.

Some churches have had a lot of success in planning special travel tours to places of historic interest in their denomination, to mission projects of the church, or even to national historic sites. These group events can help develop some deep new friendships, especially for persons who are not already active members of your church school

6. *Encourage service projects and volunteerism.* Older adults still feel they can make a helpful contribution to society. Sometimes individuals may be able to take on selected tasks within a larger project adopted by a class. For many, volunteer service is most enjoyed when done in a group of familiar friends.

This service work could have a double benefit for the Sunday school if the projects include assistance directly related to the church, such as: curtains for the nursery, writing birthday cards to children in the Sunday school, hosting a dinner for all the high school graduates, sponsoring a youth who is going through confirmation or pastor's classes, or purchasing new equipment for some classroom.

Another benefit comes when these older adults share the stories of their faith pilgrimages with the children and youth. Grandparents lose their sense of obligation to the rest of the Sunday school if their own children and grandchildren do not live in their community. A substitute grandparents program may encourage more support for the Sunday school program.

Overcoming Stumbling Blocks for Older Adults

There are a number of stumbling blocks to older adults that the church school must overcome. Leaders are often unaware of these dangers because they have become accustomed to the presence of the blocks and have unconsciously adjusted to the inconveniences they present.

Physical Barriers

While we have heard and read a lot about the ways physical barriers discourage church school attendance, we are amazingly slow at discovering ways to overcome such stumbling blocks. Too many steps, rooms that are too dark for easy reading, uncomfortable seats, and narrow passages to restrooms are all barriers for older adults.

Do not expect the older adults in your church to complain or to point out these barriers. One characteristic of older adults is the fear they are not going to be able to accomplish all they were able to do as younger persons. They have learned to be independent people and are often fearful of having to ask for help. They are reluctant to point out the places they have difficulties.

Solution: Take a walk around your church school. Check the number of steps, the distances to rooms, the lighting, etc. Better still, try making the trip in a wheelchair.

Stereotypes of Older Adults

Sometimes the self-image of older adults is damaged by all the harsh jokes and the media images portraying them. If the Sunday school complains that plans or wants are hampered by the "old-fashioned" attitudes of the senior adults, they will feel defensive and unappreciated.

Solution: Let all ages in the church find ways to express admiration and appreciation for all that their older Christian mentors have given to them. Create new intergenerational events. Have the entire church school celebrate birthdays and important anniversaries of older adults. Invite older adults to tell stories, share skills, or give service to younger persons in the church. There are lots of other ways your church school can help older adults feel appreciated.

Dwindling Circle of Friends

When older adults have been members of the same parish for a long time, the number of friends tends to dwindle and be limited to persons who are also in the same church. This discourages inviting new prospects.

Solution: Identify the kinds of acquaintances (not necessarily friends) that would be flattered by an invitation to Sunday school from an older adult. Maybe it is a clerk at the grocery store someone has talked to for ten years. It could be the receptionist at the doctor's office or a new person moved into the retirement apartments. Maybe the partner in a son's business had to move his mother in to live with him. Maybe someone recently joined the bridge club who complains that her church is too far away to attend regularly. When a widow in the church remarries, the new spouse is a good prospect.

Fear of Newcomers

This is not usually a conscious fear; it may simply be a dread of change. This fear becomes evident when the department of Christian education asks the older adult class members to move out of the classroom they have occupied for twenty years. This produces a sense of defeat if the reason given for such a forced move is that the class is now too small to warrant such a large room; a younger group needs it more than they do. It also aggravates their fear that their circle of friends is dwindling.

Solution: Always involve older adults in decisions that affect their class. Find ways to enable them to make innovative decisions for the sake of others. Cherish their feelings and honor their opinions.

Burnout

This term is not often used for older adults, but the phenomenon is present. When they are asked to take on a leadership role in the church, they often decline saying they are tired, they have done that job too long, it is time for some younger person to take over. This resistance to service may show that the older adult has been taken advantage of for years.

Solution: Sometimes prevention is the best cure to a problem. Relieve people of boring and unrewarding jobs. Excitement can be generated by a new project that captures imagination. The best solution to burnout may be a new project that people can become excited about.

Sometimes retired adults resist making commitments because they want to be free to pursue leisure activities they have long planned for in retirement. The possible solution to this problem is not to ask for help with long-range projects but only for one-time, short-term assignments. Often this reticence by a recently retired adult only lasts for a short time.

Most of these blocks to church school growth in older adults have easy, workable solutions if the church school leaders are creative and sensitive to these barriers.

Conclusion

There is no reason why the older adult classes in the church should not be able to grow as well as other ages. It could be that this group has the greatest potential for increasing attendance, especially in those parts of the country that have significant immigration of retirees.

Throughout all their years older adults have seen growth as well as decline; they have seen good times and bad; they have seen many changes, some helpful and some harmful. Older adults, therefore, are often more realistic, if not more optimistic, about the possibility for growth in the Sunday school. We could well learn from their experience.

11

Organizing for an Effective Church School

" . . . the whole body, . . . when each part is working properly, makes bodily growth and upbuilds itself in love."
—Ephesians 4:16

The dynamics of a growing Sunday School cannot be maintained with the same organizational structure year by year.
—John Sisemore[1]

The whole process of building the church school takes a conscientious effort by leaders. It is a demanding task but it promises great rewards. The major reward is bringing new persons to a commitment to Jesus Christ and full participation in the church's mission.

The preceding chapters have dealt with the work of church school teachers or age-level leaders for increasing attendance. This chapter focuses on the responsibility of the Christian education planning department, board, or committee.

Admittedly there are a few people in the church who are tired of the organizational work of the church. They dread having to attend one more meeting or to take on one more task. For these people, it may be helpful to keep in mind that the very word "administration" has within it the root word "minister." Otherwise, administration will only be a lot of menial jobs to be completed by people with little enthusiasm for the work.

There is a difference between large and small churches in their style of administration. Small churches, for example, will not feel the need to be as highly organized as many Christian education manuals suggest. Nor do they have the need for printed publicity materials. They can pass on information more efficiently by word of mouth than can a larger congregation. Large congregations, on the other hand, need extensive organization to function efficiently and definitive channels of communication to keep everyone informed.

Obviously, not all suggestions made in this chapter will be useful to every church. We hope that readers will view these suggestions for administering Christian education as idea starters and not as a list of rules that apply to everyone or every church.

Eight Stepping Stones for a Growing Church School

1. Make Christian Education the Number One Priority.

The major responsibility for administering church school is to raise the consciousness of all members of the congregation to the importance of Christian education.

a. The leaders of the ministry of Christian education must see that all the programs and future plans they hope to achieve receive adequate financial support. When the education board or council has convinced the congregation how important its work is, that congregation will see that adequate resources are available. Sometimes in the initial stages of new growth, additional fund raising methods can be useful to generate hope and enthusiasm. In the long run, however, such projects can prove to be time-consuming and draw away from the work needed in other places in the ministry.

b. The board or council of Christian education must advertise and celebrate the plans, activities, and achievements of the program of education. The larger the congregation, the less apt it is to know what is happening. Members need to be excited about the numerous achievements of the workers in the Sunday school. Smaller congregations also need such public recognition in order to feel confident that their education programs are effective.

Demonstrate to the whole church that excellence is expected in all the teachers, and then tell them how such excellence is achieved.

c. Be sure to coordinate all activities of the Sunday school with the total program of the church. Avoid schedule conflicts. Make any needed changes in the time the Sunday school meets to better address the worship needs of the church members. Change the times certain classes meet in order to prevent members from being forced to choose between an educational experience and some assigned responsibility elsewhere in the church.

It is a mistake to expect that an increase in membership and program will automatically produce a growth in stewardship. There may be as much as a three- to five-year interval between the time new members join the Sunday school and the time they begin to give their full financial support. In this initial stage of growth, the church school will have a greater strain on financial resources as program and services must increase to meet the new demand while the new financial support lags behind. When this delay occurs, many long-time parish members become frustrated and angry and question the commitment of all these new members. Such feelings are likely to occur but their effect will be lessened if leaders will celebrate the growth and achievements.

2. Select Programs That Are Likely to Produce Growth.

a. Involve the whole congregation in defining what it wants to accomplish in its Christian education ministry. Write out the goals or make a mission statement for the church school. This discipline will develop greater support within the church. It can also make the work of administering the program easier; leaders can concentrate on those programs that the congregation values and no longer struggle with things that need not be important.

b. Evaluate all the procedures, classes, and special programs to see whether or not they set a style of openness to newcomers, inclusiveness of all people, and willingness for change.

c. See that all teachers and leaders in the program feel a sense of achievement and satisfaction, that they personally contribute to the church school's goal of making disciples.

3. Train Teachers How to Increase the Attendance.

See that each church school teacher is properly prepared to do his or her job well. Teachers should feel competent and effective. Most church school curriculum resources provide basic teaching skills like lesson planning, understanding age-level development, and using creative learning activities. Although some materials have suggestions for increasing church school attendance, teachers may need more help in this area than the curriculum can provide.

a. Teachers need to know the importance of developing a personal relationship with each person. Only when pupils feel they truly belong will they be ready for effective learning. In Assemblies of God church schools (the fastest growing schools over the last decade), each classroom teacher is expected to make *one* personal contact by visit or telephone *each* week with *each* pupil and *each* visitor. No doubt this practice has had a great impact on Sunday school growth. It demonstrates that the teachers care about their students.

b. Teachers need to train pupils to articulate the meaning and content of their faith to persons who are not in the church. Teachers of youth and adults can do this by discussion methods. Teachers of children can train them to express their faith by using role play, simulations, and case studies.

c. Each teacher should be provided with attendance boosters for the classroom. These might include class rosters, attendance charts, photos of each pupil to display, telephone contact suggestions, cards to mail to students who have missed, thank you notes, attendance awards, and birthday and congratulations cards.

4. Set Attendance Goals That Are Achievable

The purpose of attendance goals is to make the congregation aware of the importance of looking for new prospects for Sunday school. Remember not to make these goals too grandiose; if one fails, the result could be defeat and discouragement. Celebrate every evidence of growth, no matter how small.

Attendance goals in the children's classes will teach them that they are responsible for inviting non-churched persons into the church. Such evangelism is an important task of each person who seeks to live a Christian life; it is as important as prayer, personal spiritual disciplines, stewardship, and service to the poor.

Attendance goals for adult classes are also important. Adults, however, have some strong memories of their own childhood years in Sunday school and may be skeptical of anything that smacks of the attendance contests of those early years. Goals that best apply to adult classes are those that deal with starting new classes and how many new visitors can be attracted within a six- or twelve-month period.

Growth often occurs in a snowball fashion, beginning with a very small clump. It takes a long time before growth begins to accumulate to the point that it is noticeable to the rest of the church. Sometimes growth exhibits itself first by the current pupils simply increasing the frequency of their attendance.

5. Select Relevant Curriculum and Provide Quality Resources.

Here are a few questions that might help your board of Christian education assess whether your curriculum and other teaching resources are likely to enhance church school growth:

—Are the Bibles provided in each age level appropriate to the reading skills of that level? Are they neat and in good repair? Is the print large enough to be read by all pupils?
—Does the curriculum encourage the teacher/leader to call for conversion of some unchurched members as well as for the personal growth and development of current members?
—Does the curriculum address the personal life concerns of those outside the church as well as those of your current members? Does it call for members to practice outreach and service as well as to grow in their faith?
—Does the church school provide adequate back-up resources for each class that reflect the ways people learn in today's society? Does each room have adequate equipment?

6. Reorganize as the Sunday School Grows.

In order to implement some of the suggestions made in this book, it may be necessary to reorganize the congregation's Christian education department or board. It may also be necessary to abandon some old programs in order to give people time and resources to follow stepping stones to growth.

a. The simplest way to start change is to add new people to initiate some of the ideas suggested in this book. More persons may be needed to help with attendance records and fellowship events outside of classroom time. Recruit some greeters and someone who will design and have printed a brochure that describes the Christian education program.

b. Eliminate those tasks that are not needed any longer, especially those that tend to prevent growth. Maybe the classroom teachers could organize and stock the education supplies while the person formerly responsible might organize greeters or make new directional signs.

c. Include newcomers or new members by recruiting them for jobs that are clear and simple, ones for which the new person is likely to succeed. Choose tasks that increase attendance or follow-up on dropouts.

d. Include new persons in committee meetings; they will add a fresh set of ideas to the work. Watch for discouragement and burnout in long-time church members who feel that they have been passed over or forced out of those leadership roles in which they once found much personal pride.

e. Keep in mind that the larger the church school becomes the more the committees will need to rely upon printed minutes, written meeting notices, and copies of publicity materials. The larger the Sunday school, the more time needed for record keeping.

7. Review the building for its impact on visitors.

It takes the entire department, council, or board of Christian education to address this issue. Review the principles of church school growth outlined in chapter 3. Take the newest member of the church on a tour of the halls and classrooms of the church to look for its positive or negative impact on a visitor or newcomer. Better still, request some friend who is not a member of your church, or an active leader in some other church, to help.

Here are some questions to ask about your church school facility:

—Does it need new paint?
—Do the bulletin boards need to be lowered to the proper height for children?
—Do outmoded light fixtures make rooms seem gloomy?
—Should the artwork and pictures on the wall be replaced by more colorful, more religious, or more contemporary pictures?
—Does the teacher need more storage space so that the room looks ready for class and not cluttered with Christmas decor in May?

Planners must always be prepared to reassign classroom space as attendance changes. This can sometimes be a minefield—especially when dealing with some adult classes. It is wise to involve them in the decision-making.

Be sure there are adequate parking spaces for visitors. Sometimes a reminder to leave the spots that are closest to the church door for visitors will help current church members to realize the importance of being prepared to greet and welcome newcomers. Some congregations even mark a few places as reserved for visitors.

Provide lots of information for visitors: schedules for classes and other church activities, dates for important church events, and times for all programs. While some small churches will feel that such material is not necessary, they will do well to invent some method of letting visitors know these details in time for them to decide if they want to participate. Often, take-home materials are best for the newcomer so that they are able to check information when they have questions later. Visitors are usually barraged with a lot of new information on their first visit, and they will not be able to remember all the details.

8. Be Sure the Pastor Is Supportive of Education.

Remind the pastor of his or her historic priestly function as a teacher or rabbi, a pastoral role long neglected by some pastors who want to serve as a theologian-in-residence. They may need to be reminded that the best educational methods begin where the learner is and not where professionals insist they ought to be.

Recognize and appreciate the pastor who is already a teacher. In growing church schools, pastors teach a regular learning group. The smaller the congregation, the more apt the pastor is to be the church school teacher of a youth or adult class as well as the primary director of the entire educational program. Encourage the pastor to be the counselor and supporter of all teachers and leaders in the educational ministry. In larger congregations that have more staff persons, the senior pastor may feel that education is the responsibility of some other person. Yet if the pastor is not an enthusiastic crusader for education and personal growth in faith, the church school will have difficulty growing. Involve the pastor in all the goal setting and long-range planning for the program of Christian education. It will encourage the pastor to have greater commitment to seeing that those goals are achieved.

Christian education committees often rely upon the pastor to make the announcements about their programs in the parish newsletter, the worship bulletin, and during the Sunday worship service. Encourage her or him to include the plans for new programs, upcoming events, and recognition and celebration of the achievements of educational ministry. Some pastors are also very adept at getting news of their congregation into the local media.

Another practical help from the pastor is the sharing of the names of prospects and visitors for the church school. Such prospects can come from new couples who were counseled before marriage, visitors to the worship services of the church, newcomers who have moved into the community, members of the extended families of church members whom the pastor has met during times of illness or at funerals.

Whatever the blocks, there are some solutions in this book that can be a real help to one's church school. There are a lot of facts and new information that can begin to change some negative attitudes. There are several principles that can be a framework for a new perspective on our mutual work. And there are a few pithy comments that might provide some new motivation for our work.

Christian education commitment is a very fine way to fulfill Christ's command to "Go therefore and make disciples, . . . teaching them to observe all that I have commanded you." Draw power from the promise that accompanied that command, "I am with you always, to the close of the age" (Matthew 28:20).

Appendix A

Stepping Stones for Church School Growth

A church school will grow that
- —believes that growth is possible and appropriate.
- —places high value on the importance of Christian education.
- —is able to say "who it is" in a winsome and inviting manner.
- —helps persons feel they belong and their presence is prized.
- —seeks new members through friendship and kinship ties of current members.
- —takes seriously the spiritual growth and personal life concerns of all people.
- —has easy access for newcomers and provides a welcoming environment.
- —provides quality programs.
- —is able to open new entrances into the church while reducing the number of exits.
- —welcomes new members, accepts the changes they bring, and assimilates those new members into the leadership of the church.

Fifteen First Steps for Increasing Church School Attendance

1. Set goals
2. Keep attendance records
3. Develop a list of prospects
4. Let newcomers tell the story
5. Train members how to invite
6. Use greeters at each entrance
7. Follow up on all visitors
8. Use name tags
9. Start new classes
10. Have leaders prepared
11. Reduce physical barriers
12. Use lots of signs
13. Provide ample parking
14. Advertise in church
15. Advertise in your community

Appendix B

Appendix B

Organizing for an Effective Church School

1. Make Christian education the number one priority by
—providing adequate financial support.
—advertising and celebrating your achievements.
—coordinating with all other church programs.

2. Select programs that will produce church school growth by
—involving the whole congregation in goal-setting.
—seeing that all church programs are "open" to newcomers.

3. Train church school teachers how to increase the attendance by
—developing personal rapport with each pupil.
—training pupils to share their faith with others.
—providing resources for attendance boosters.

4. Set attendance goals that are achievable; celebrate success.

5. Select relevant curriculum and provide quality resources.

6. Reorganize your structure as your church school grows by
—adding new department members to assume new tasks
—eliminating those tasks that have outlived their usefulness.
—finding ways to include the newcomers in planning.
—as your Sunday school gets larger, providing more information in printed form rather than relying upon word of mouth.

7. Review your building for its impact on visitors.

8. Be sure the pastor is supportive of education.

Notes

Chapter 1: A New Day Is Dawning for the Church School

1. *1985 Yearbook of American and Canadian Churches,* published by the National Council of Churches, reported by Religious News Services, n.d.
2. Research of Harold Johnson, from the *1986 Year Book of The Christian Church (Disciples of Christ)* reported in *The Christian Church of Greater Kansas City.* Vol. 12, No. 11 (September 1987), p. 11.
3. Kate Greer, "Are American Families Finding New Strength in Spirituality?" *Better Homes and Gardens,* January, 1988, pp. 16-27.
4. Lyle Schaller, "The Contemporary Religious Revival." *The Parish Paper,* 1981, p. 2.

Chapter 2: Restoring the Partnership of Education and Evangelism

1. George Sweazy, *Effective Evangelism* (1953) quoted in Kendig Brubaker Cully, ed., *The Westminster Dictionary of Christian Education.* Westminster Press, 1963, p. 241.
2. John H. Westerhoff, III., "A Necessary Paradox: Catechesis and Evangelism; Nurture and Conversion." *Religious Education Journal,* Vol. LXXIII, No. 4 (July-August 1978), p. 412.
3. Win Arn. "The Sunday School—A Method in Search of a Mission" *The Win Arn Growth Report,* No. 19, pp. 1, 2.
4. J. Cy Rowell, *Foundational Aims of Christian Education for the Christian Church (Disciples of Christ).* CBP Press, n.d., p. 3.
5. *Ibid.,* p. 8.
6. *The Educational Mission of the United Church of Christ.* The United Church Board for Homeland Ministries, 1988, p. 6.
7. *A Stance Toward the Future—The Mission of Joint Educational Development.* Joint Educational Development, 1986, p. 4.
8. David L. Bartlett and Ruth Fowler, *Moments of Commitment: Years of Growth.* CBP Press, 1987, p. 39.
9. John Westerhoff, "Formation, Education, Instruction." *Religious Education,* Vol. 82, No. 4 (Fall 1987), pp. 582-588.
10. *Ibid.,* p. 585.
11. Maria Harris, *Teaching and Religious Imagination.* Harper and Row, 1987, p. 94.
12. Westerhoff, "A Necessary Paradox," p. 412.
13. Bartlett and Fowler, *Moments of Commitment,* p. 29.

Chapter 3: Principles for Church School Growth

1. G.W. Garvin, "Marks of Growing Churches." *Action Information,* Vol. XI, No. 5 (September/October 1985), p. 1.
2. See Herb Miller, *How to Build a Magnetic Church.* Abingdon Press, 1987, p.3.

155

3. Herb Miller, "'Mainline Growth' Workshop Told Must Gain Commitment to Christ." *The National Christian Reporter*, September 20, 1985, p. 4.
4. Willmar Thorkelson, "Loving Churches Are Growing Churches." *The National Christian Reporter*, Vol. 6, No. 35 (October 31, 1986), p. 4.
5. Miller, *How to Build a Magnetic Church*, p. 31.
6. Lyle Schaller, "Seven Trends That Are Shaping Church Life." *Presbyterian Survey*, Vol 72, No. 1 (January 1982), p. 36.
7. Miller, *How to Build a Magnetic Church,* pp. 72-73.

Chapter 4: Roadblocks, Detours, and Barriers
1. Kenneth D. Blazier, *A Growing Church School*. Judson Press, 1978, p.12.
2. R.W. Gibbons, "New Hints About Ministry with the Baby Boom Generation." *Action Information,* Vol. XII, No. 2 (March/April 1986), Alban Institute, p. 18.
3.*The Connecticut Mutual Life Report on American Values in the 1980s: The Impact of Belief,* 1981.

Chapter 7: Youth
1. "Youth Reaching for Spiritual Growth." *Net Results*, December, 1986, p. 6.
2. *Group Magazine,* Box 202, Mt. Morris, IL, 61054.

Chapter 8: The Young Adult
1. Miller, "Mainline Growth Workshop," p. 4.
2. "Gallup: Percentage of 'Unchurched' Rising," report on *The Unchurched American*. Religious News Service, n.d.
3. David Alderfer and Arvid Anderson, *The Baby Boom Generation in Congregations of the Lutheran Church in America.* Division for Parish Services, Lutheran Church in America, 1986, p. 19.
4. R. T. Gribbon, *30 Year Olds and the Church: Ministry with the Baby Boom Generation.* Alban Institute, p. 1.
5. Research of William McKinney and David Roozen reported in *Keeping You Posted*. Office of Communication, United Church of Christ, Vol. 22, No. 2 (February 1987), p. 3.
6. Gribbon, *30 Year Olds,* pp. 4ff.
7. The research of Ralph Whitehead, Jr., of the University of Massachusetts, reported by Jon Stewart, "Words by Wire." *The St. Louis Post-Dispatch,* 1987.
8. Alderfer and Anderson, *The Baby Boom Generation,* pp. 22ff.
9. Lyle E. Schaller, *It's a Different World.* Abingdon Press, 1987, p. 31.
10. Gribbon, *30 Year Olds,* p. 13.
11. Herb Miller, *Tools for Active Christians.* CBP Press, 1979, pp. 67 ff.

Chapter 9: Middle Adults
1. Schaller, "Seven Trends," p. 36.

Chapter 10: Older Adults
1. Charles L. Allen and Mildred Parker, *How to Increase Your Sunday School Attendance.* Fleming H. Revell, 1980, p. 78.
2. Lyle Schaller, "Questions for the Futures Committee." *The Parish Paper*, 1988, p. 2.
3. Bruce W. Berry, *Evaluating Your Ministry To, For and With Older Adults.* The Missouri Office of Aging, n.d., p.3.

Chapter 11: Organizing for an Effective Church School
1. John T. Sisemore, *Church Growth Through the Sunday School.* Broadman Press, 1983, p 29.

Bibliography

Alderfer, David and Arvid Anderson, *The Baby Boom Generation in the Congregations of the Lutheran Church in America.* Division of Parish Services, Lutheran Church in America (1986), p. 19.

Allen, Charles and Mildred Parker, *How to Increase Your Sunday School Attendance.* Old Tappan, New Jersey: Fleming H. Revell, n.d.

Arn, Charles, D. McGavran, and W. Arn, *Growth: A New Vision for the Sunday School.* Pasadena: Church Growth Press, 1980.

Arn, Win, "The Sunday School—A Method in Search of a Mission." *The Win Arn Growth Report,* No. 19, n.d., pp. 1, 2.

"Assemblies Sunday School Success Secrets Are Told." *The National Christian Reporter,* Vol. 3, No. 29 (September 23, 1983), p. 2.

Bartlett, David L. and Ruth Fowler, *Moments of Commitment: Years of Growth.* St. Louis: CBP Press, 1987.

Benedict, James, "Church Growth, Beating the Odds." *Resources,* Alban Institute (Spring, 1989), pp. 12, 13.

Berry, Bruce, "Evaluating Your Ministry To, For and With Older Adults." The Missouri Office of Aging, n.d., p. 6.

Blazier, Kenneth D., *A Growing Church School.* Valley Forge: Judson Press, n.d.

Callahan, Kennon, *Twelve Keys to an Effective Church.* San Francisco: Harper & Row, 1983.

Christian Church of Greater Kansas City, The, Vol. 12, No. 11 (September 1987), p. 11.

Clapp, Steve, *Christian Education as Evangelism.* C4 Resources, n.d.

"Connecticut Mutual Life Report on American Values in the 1980s: The Impact of Belief." 1981.

Cully, Kendig Brubaker ed., *The Westminster Dictionary of Christian Education.* Philadelphia: The Westminster Press, 1963.

Educational Mission of the United Church of Christ, The. The United Church of Christ Board for Homeland Ministries, 1988.

"Gallup: Percentage of Unchurched Rising." Religious News Service, n.d.

Garvin, G.W., "Marks of Growing Churches." *Action Information,* Vol. XI, No. 5 (September/October 1985), p. 1.

Gibbons, R.W., "New Hints About Ministry with the Baby Boom Generation." *Action Information,* Vol. XII, No. 2 (March/April 1986), p. 18.

Goodson, Millie, *Sunday School Growth and Renewal: How to Reach, Teach, Care, Share.* Nashville: Discipleship Resources, 1984.

Greer, Kate, "Are American Families Finding New Strength in Spirituality?" *Better Homes and Gardens* (January 1988), pp. 16-27.

Gribbon, R.T., *30 Year Olds and the Church: Ministry with the Baby Boom Generation.* The Alban Insitutue, n.d., p. 1.

———, *When People Seek the Church.* The Alban Institute, n.d., pp. 13-20.

Harris, Maria, *Teaching and Religious Imagination.* San Francisco: Harper & Row, 1987.

Hartman, Warren and Roy Ryan, "Evangelism Through the Church School."
    Course guide by Discipleship Resources, n.d., p. 3.
Miller, Herb, *How to Build a Magnetic Church*. Nashville: Abingdon Press,
    1987.
————"'Mainline Growth' Workshop Told Must Gain Commitment to
    Christ." *The National Christian Reporter* (September 20, 1985),
    p. 4.
————*Tools for Active Christians.* St. Louis: CBP Press, 1979.
Murray, Dick, *Strengthening the Adult Sunday School Class.* Nashville:
    Abingdon Press, 1981
Net Results, Vol. 1, No. 9 (April 1981), p. 3.
1985 Yearbook of American and Canadian Churches, National Council of
    Churches.
O'Neal, Debbie, *Handbook for Church Nurseries.* Minneapolis: Augsburg,
    1985.
Ostling, Richard N., "Those Mainline Blues." *Time,* Vol. 133, No. 21 (May
    22, 1989), p. 95.
Proctor, Frank, "Matching Training to Teachers' Level of Experience." *JED
    Share,* Vol. 11, No. 3 (Fall 1982), pp. 20-21.
————"What Motivates Leaders." *Vanguard* (October/November/ Decem-
    ber 1981), p. 7.
Rowell, J. Cy, *Foundational Aims of Christian Education.* St. Louis: CBP
    Press, n.d.
Schaller, Lyle, "The Contemporary Religious Revival." *The Parish Paper*
    (1981), p. 2.
————, "The Growing Shortage of Grandparents." *The Parish Paper*
    (1983), p. 2.
————*It's a Different World.* Nashville: Abingdon Press, 1987.
————"Questions for the Futures Committee." *The Parish Paper* (1988),
    p. 2.
————"Seven Trends That Are Shaping Church Life." *Presbyterian Sur-
    vey,* Vol. 72, No. 1 (January 1982), p. 36.
————"We Are Growing Older." *The Parish Paper* (1984), p. 1.
————"Where Do People Go to Church?" *The Parish Paper* (1988), p. 2.
————"Where Have All the Men Gone?" *Presbyterian Survey,* Vol. 72,
    No. 8 (September 1982), p. 20.
Sisemore, John, *Church Growth Through the Sunday School.* Nashville:
    Broadman Press, 1983.
Sprinkle, Patricia H., "Is Your Church Flunking Crib Evangelism?" *The
    Disciple* (September 1988), p. 38.
Stance Toward the Future—The Mission of Joint Educational Development."
    Joint Educational Development, 1986, p. 3.
Stewart, Jon, "Words by Wire." *The St. Louis Post Dispatch,* 1987.
Sunday School Growth Kit Sampler,The. Nashville: Abingdon Press,
    1985.
"Survey Finds Baby Boomers Are Coming Back to Church." *Keeping You
    Posted,* Office ofCommunication, United Church of Christ, Vol. 22,
    No. 2 (February 1987), p. 3.

268
P964

LINCOLN CHRISTIAN COLLEGE AND SEMINARY

8372

160   *Bibliography*

Thorkelson, Willmar, "Loving Churches Are Growing Churches." *The National Christian Reporter*, Vol. 6, No. 35 (October 31, 1986), p. 4.

"Unchurched American, The." Study Conducted for the Religious Coalition to Study Backgrounds, Values and Interests of Unchurched Americans. National Council of Churches of Christ in the U.S.A., 1978.

Westerhoff, John H. III, "Formation, Education, Instruction." *Religious Education*, Vol. 82, No. 4 (Fall 1987), pp. 582-588.

———"A Necessary Paradox: Catechesis and Evangelism; Nurture and Conversion." *Religious Education Journal*, Vol. LXXIII, No. 4 (July-August 1978), p. 412.

———*Will Our Children Have Faith?* Winston-Seabury Press, 1976.

"What's in Store for United States Population Trends in the 1980's?" *Cutting Edge*, Vol. II, No. 4 (July-August 1982), pp. 1, 2.

Williams, Cleophas, "Our Growing Sunday School." *The Church School Today*, Vol. 6, No. 3, Part 1 (Winter 1987-88), Graded Press, p. 8.

Wycoff, D. Campbell, "As American as Crabgrass: The Protestant Sunday School." *ACCENotes*, Vol. 15, No. 11 (September 1982), p. 11.

Youth Reaching for Spiritual Growth." *Net Results* (December 1986), p. 6.

Zehring, John W., "How to Train the Members." *Yokefellow Institute News* (Winter, 1983), p. 7.

3 4711 00181 0862